The complete guide to the

Feng Shui GARDEN

The complete guide to the

Feng Shui GARDEN

GILL HALE

HERMES HOUSE

This edition is published by Hermes House

Hermes House is an imprint of Anness Publishing Ltd
Hermes House, 88–89 Blackfriars Road, London SE1 8HA
tel. 020 7401 2077; fax 020 7633 9499; info@anness.com

A CIP catalogue record for this book is available from the British Library.

Publisher: Joanna Lorenz
Senior Editor: Joanne Rippin
Designer: Nigel Partridge
Special Photography: John Freeman
Stylist: Claire Hunt
Illustrator: Geoff Ball
Editorial Reader: Richard McGinlay

(for picture acknowledgements see page 94)

1 3 5 7 9 10 8 6 4 2

CONTENTS

INTRODUCTION

Feng Shui is basically an environmental science and its origins are simple. It is based on the ancient Chinese interpretation of the natural world, and on observation of the movement of the heavenly bodies to determine the passage of time. In the modern world, the natural processes at work in the garden allow us to remain in touch with nature and with the eternal rhythms of the universe. Gardeners are in a special position, in that they work with the earth and the energy from the heavens.

As practised today, Feng Shui gives us advice on how to create environments in which we feel comfortable. Some of the principles of Feng Shui stem from the culture and mythology of China, though many are echoed in what is considered to be good garden design all around the world. The intention of this book is to encourage gardeners to incorporate features from their own culture, and to plan a garden according to principles that preserve the spirit and traditions of its situation. Feng Shui allows for cultural differences.

With an understanding of the principles of Feng Shui, we can choose garden features which are harmonious and which can help to create a balanced and supportive place. A Feng Shui garden also allows for individualism and does not preclude "statements" in design or planting which clash with accepted norms. In fact, such clashes can often create a vibrant and challenging energy which can help us to develop at certain times in our lives. A Feng Shui garden reflects the seasons and is designed for year-round interest. The leafless canopy of a deciduous tree against the sky in winter, or an interesting autumn seedhead, can be just as beautiful as a mass of flowers. The plants we grow can feed all our senses with their colour, form, textures and smells, and this is important in a Feng Shui garden.

The conditions in which we grow the plants are crucial if they are to be healthy and take their place happily in the garden's eco-system. A healthy soil produces healthy plants and supports millions of micro-organisms, each of which has a role to play. Healthy plants support wildlife, and even those species we consider undesirable will provide food for those we welcome into our gardens. If we try to fight the natural energies of the garden, or exert too much control, we will create unhealthy imbalances. A correct balance of plants, growing in ground conditions to which they are best suited, planted at the prime time to support their growth habits, is the key to creating a truly harmonious garden that will support and nourish the senses.

Modern lifestyles leave us little time to stop and consider the effect our surroundings have on our health and on our peace of mind. However, even if we live in a city, we can leave the stressful urban lifestyle behind us as we enter the tranquillity of the garden – even if it is only a tiny space in a basement or on a balcony. There is an increasing awareness that some aspects of modern technology can create lasting damage to the planet. Although this is not Feng Shui in its purest form, concern for our environment and an awareness of the damage we inflict on it must form part of Feng Shui for the present age. The use of chemicals in a Feng Shui garden is not to be recommended since they degrade the soil and kill useful insects as well as those we consider to be pests. Careful planting and an awareness of the relationships between plants will enable us to create gardens where spraying is unnecessary.

The intention of this book is to interpret Feng Shui for modern times and modern gardeners without straying from its underlying principles. Feng Shui offers us the opportunity to achieve health, happiness and well-being by living in harmony with our environment.

WHAT IS FENG SHUI?

The Chinese have a saying, "First, luck; second, destiny; third, Feng Shui; fourth, virtues; fifth, education": although Feng Shui can be a powerful force in shaping our lives, it is not a cure for all ills. Luck plays a major role, and personality, or karma, is almost as important. What we do with our lives and how we behave towards others will play a part, and education gives us the tools to make sense of the world. Feng Shui is just one part of the complete package.

▲ *In China the dragon symbolizes good fortune. Its presence is felt in landforms and watercourses.*

▲ *The Dragon Hills which protect Hong Kong are believed to be responsible for its prosperity.*

► *Much of the symbolic imagery in Feng Shui is taken from landscapes such as this in Guilin, southern China.*

The single factor which sets Feng Shui apart from other philosophical systems is that it has the capacity for change built into it. Most systems evolved from similar principles; understanding the natural world played a major role and natural phenomena were believed to be imbued with a spirit or deity, recognition of which would give people some benefit in their lives. Where these systems became established as religions, the deities were worshipped, but Feng Shui has remained a philosophy and can be used in any culture and alongside any belief system.

Feng Shui uses formulae which determine the rising and falling energy in a given time span of an individual or a house. Other formulae indicate a person's best location within a home or office, and can suggest the best placing of beds and desks. Many Chinese people consult astrologers annually to further refine this, so that every activity within the year can be pinpointed accurately and undertaken at an auspicious time. This can be as precise as the best time to conceive or even when to wash your hair.

The philosophy of Feng Shui is embraced by people who are aware of the impact their surroundings have on them and feel the need to take action to improve their lives, but using Feng Shui correctly is a skill and its principles cannot be adapted simply to suit the circumstances of a place or an individual.

Feng Shui enables us to position ourselves within our environment to our best advantage. The positioning of our houses and offices as well as their internal design affects each of us positively or negatively. Feng Shui helps us to determine the most favourable positions for us and the layouts, colours and designs which will support us. In the garden we can determine the best locations for the different activities we intend to pursue there, but we also have to take account of the plants in the garden and their needs, which are equally important if the environment is to thrive.

▲ *Water energy plays a significant role in Feng Shui. Here a fountain brings life to an office courtyard.*

The following chapters provide information on those aspects of this complex and fascinating subject that can be utilized by everyone in their own space. When we introduce Feng Shui into our lives we can only benefit, even where we only touch the surface. As we become more aware of our surroundings, and actively begin to change those factors with which we feel uncomfortable, we begin to gain a deeper insight into ourselves and our part in the wider picture.

▼ *Our surroundings affect us. Fresh air, natural products and a healthy environment enhance our mental and physical well-being.*

▼ *The T'ung Shui almanac, produced for centuries, details the best times to move house, conceive and even wash your hair.*

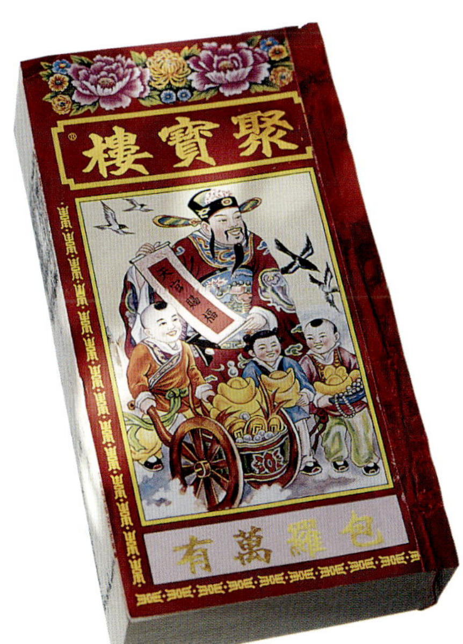

APPROACHES TO FENG SHUI

Feng Shui is about interpreting environments. Practitioners use a number of different approaches to connect with the energy or "feel" of a place, and fine-tune it to make it work for those living or working there. Provided the principles are understood, the different approaches will be effective. More often than not, practitioners use a mixture of methods to create the effects they want.

The Environmental Approach

In ancient times, people lived by their wits and knowledge of local conditions. Their needs were basic: food and shelter. Observation would tell them from which direction the prevailing winds were coming and they would build their homes in protective sites. They needed water in order to grow and transport their crops so rivers were important, and the direction of the flow and the orientation of the banks would determine the type of crops which could be grown. This branch of Feng Shui is known as the Form or Landform School and was the earliest approach to the subject.

▼ *The Form School regards this as the ideal spot on which to build. The Black Tortoise hill at the rear offers support while the White Tiger and Green Dragon give protection from the wind, with the all-powerful dragon slightly higher than the Tiger. The Red Phoenix marks the front boundary, and the river irrigates the site and enables crops to be transported for trade.*

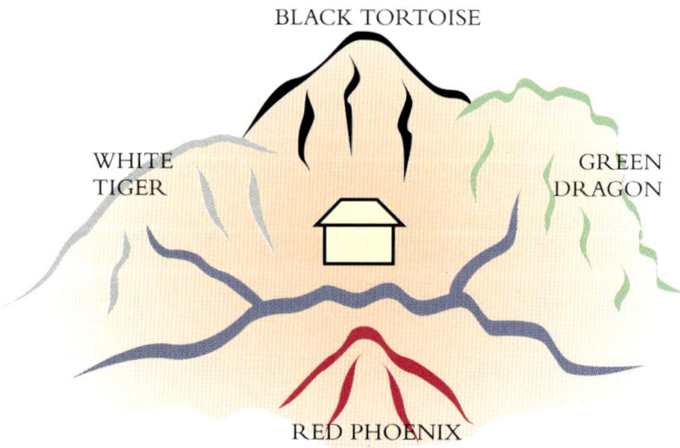

▲ *These "Karst" limestone hills in China symbolically protect an area of rich agricultural land.*

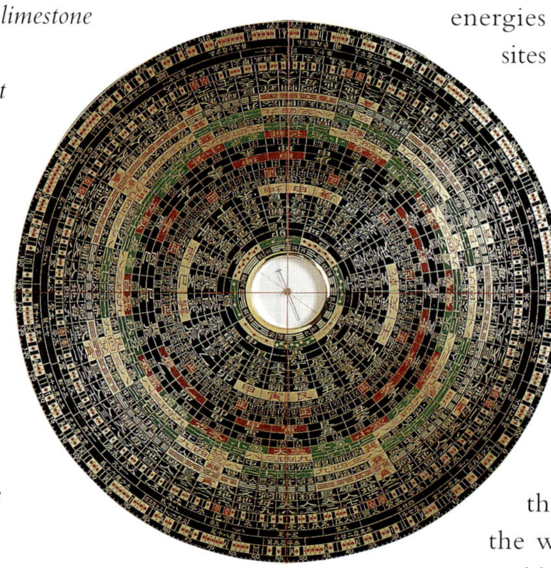

► *A luo pan or compass, used by geomancers in ancient China. Much of the information it records is regularly used by Feng Shui consultants.*

The Compass Approach

In ancient China, geomancers investigated earth formations and watercourses while astronomers charted the skies. Those who understood the power of the information they possessed recorded their knowledge on an instrument called a luo pan, or compass. The luo pan illustrates not only direction, but also investigates the energy of each direction, depending on the landform or heavenly body to be found there. Interpreting these energies suggests suitable sites for human beings. Feng Shui is based on the *I Ching*, a philosophical book which interprets the energies of the universe. Its 64 images from the yearly nature cycle form the outer ring of the luo pan. With the wisdom of ancient sages added to it over the centuries, the *I Ching* offers us a means to connect to the natural flow of the universe. Its built-in time factor allows individuals to connect to it in different ways at different times in their lives.

The Intuitive Approach

Ancient texts illustrate every shape of mountain and watercourse. The names illustrate concepts significant to the Chinese psyche. "Tiger in Waiting" suggests a negative place, where residents will never be able to relax, whereas "Baby Dragon Looking at its Mother" indicates a much more restful environment.

The ancient text of the *Water Dragon Classic* provides more information on the best places to build, showing flow direction and position within the tributaries, with the names again indicating the type of environment. The sensibilities of people living and working on the land were finely tuned and their knowledge of the natural world endowed them with an instinct for suitable sites to grow crops.

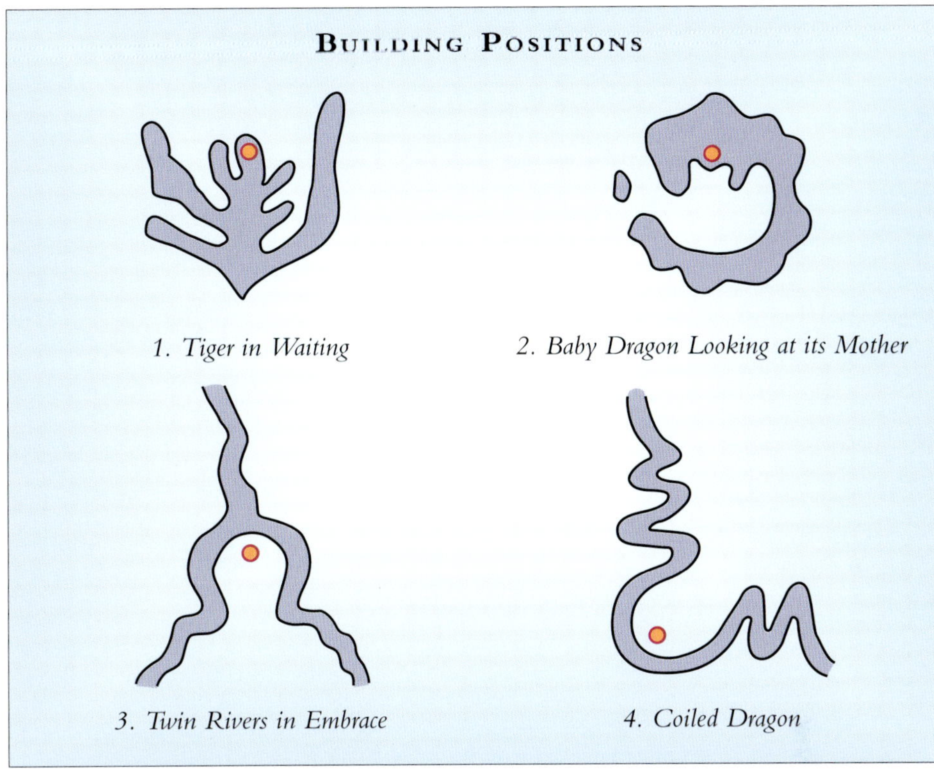

► *Mountain sites (1 & 2) and river sites (3 & 4); the dots represent buildings. All except for "Tiger in Waiting" are auspicious positions to build a new home.*

▼ *This prime site is protected by mountains, with healthy watercourses.*

THE PRINCIPLES OF FENG SHUI

Ancient peoples regarded the heavens, the earth and themselves as part of one system. This holistic view of life persists in many cultures, where health and medicine, food and lifestyle, and the route to salvation are all interconnected in one ecological system.

The Way

The Tao, or the Way, the philosophy of which underlies Feng Shui, shows how to order our lives to live in harmony with ourselves, each other and the natural world. We can use Feng Shui to help us work towards achieving this.

Yin and Yang

Positive and negative forces act together in order to create energy – in electricity, for instance. Yin and Yang represent these two forces which are in constant movement, each attempting to gain dominance. Where one achieves dominance, an imbalance occurs, so when one force becomes too strong its influence subsides and the other takes over. Still water, for example, is yin; a raging torrent is yang. Imagine a slow-moving yin river. When it hits rocks and descends, turbulence occurs, it speeds up and becomes yang. When it flows into a lake, it slows down and becomes yin once more. Yin and yang are opposing but interdependent concepts – without the idea of cold we would not be able to describe heat. At their extremes they

▲ *The T'ai Chi symbol illustrates the concept of yin and yang, the opposite yet interdependent forces that drive the world.*

◀ *Circle, Square, Triangle – signifying Heaven, Earth, human beings – the universal cosmological symbol.*

▼ *"The Dragon Breathing on the Lake" – the lake is a powerful Chinese image, symbolizing a light-reflective surface harbouring a dark and deep interior.*

YIN	YANG
Moon	Sun
Winter	Summer
Dark	Light
Feminine	Masculine
Interior	Exterior
Low	High
Stillness	Movement
Passive	Active
Odd numbers	Even numbers
Earth	Heaven
Cold	Heat
Soft	Hard
Valleys	Hills
Still water	Mountains
Gardens	Houses
Sleep	Wakefulness

change into each other; ice can burn and sunstroke sufferers shiver. The aim is to achieve a balance between them. There are examples throughout the book of how we can achieve this in our own environments. Some of the more common associations are listed left.

CHI

Chi is a concept unknown in Western philosophy but figures repeatedly in the philosophies of the East. It is the life force of all animate things, the quality of environments, the power of the sun, the moon and weather systems, and the driving force in human beings. In China, the movements in T'ai Chi encourage chi to move through the body. Acupuncture needles are used to unblock its flow when stuck. Chinese herbal medicine uses the special energetic qualities of herbs to correct chi when it becomes unbalanced. Meditation helps to establish a healthy mind: every brush stroke of the Chinese artist or sweep of the calligrapher's pen is the result of trained mental processes and the correct breathing techniques, which ensure that each carefully composed painting or document is infused with chi.

▼ *An acupuncturist at work. The needles unblock the energy channels and enable chi to flow round the body.*

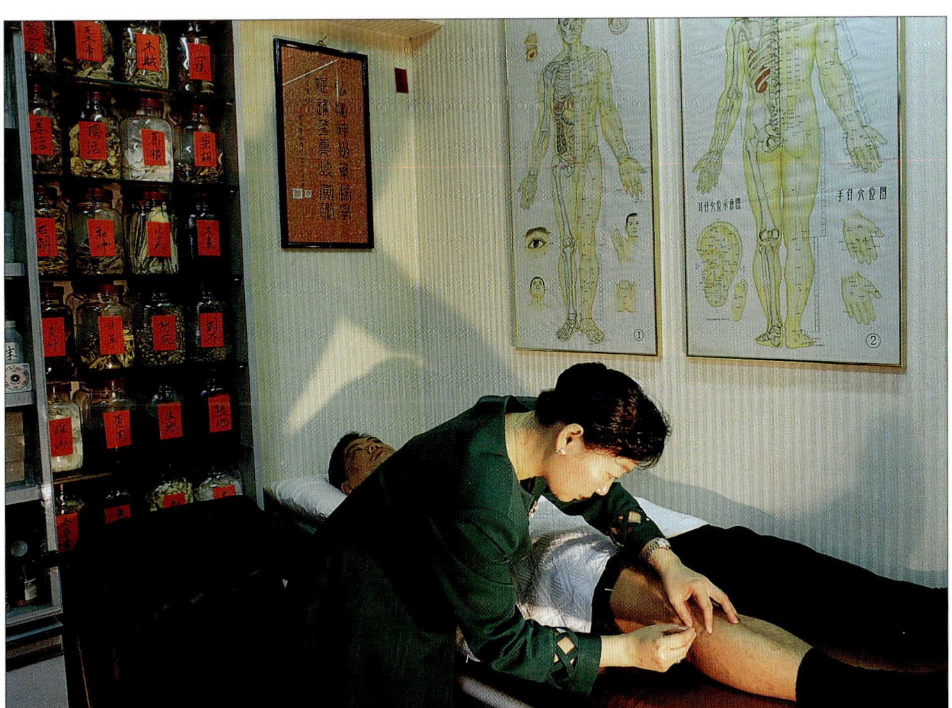

▲ *Chinese people practising T'ai Chi. The exercises are designed to aid the flow of chi in the body.*

The purpose of Feng Shui is to create environments in which chi flows smoothly to achieve physical and mental health. Where chi flows gently through a house, the occupants will be positive and will have an easy passage through life. Where chi moves sluggishly or becomes stuck, then the chances are that problems will occur in the day-to-day life or long-term prospects of those living there.

Where chi flows smoothly in the garden, the plants will be healthy and the wildlife there will flourish. Animals, birds, insects and the myriad of unseen micro-organisms that live there will regulate themselves and create a balanced and supportive environment. Where chi cannot flow unimpeded and becomes sluggish or stuck, an area may become dank or there may be an imbalance which creates, say, a plague of aphids.

In an office where chi flows freely, employees will be happy and supportive, projects will be completed on time and stress levels will be low. Where the chi is stuck, there will be disharmony and the business will not flourish.

FIVE TYPES OF ENERGY

Some of the latest scientific theories enable us to make sense of the ancient formulae on which Feng Shui is based. It is accepted that everything in the universe vibrates. All our senses and everything we encounter are attuned to certain frequencies, which react with us in a positive or negative way. We are all familiar with sound waves, which bring us radio, and electromagnetic waves, which bring us television. Colours, shapes, food, weather conditions – everything in our lives affects us on a vibrational level for good or ill and, in turn, we react in various yet predictable ways, depending on our individual traits.

The concept of elements exists throughout the world. The Chinese recognize five which arise out of the interplay of yin and yang and represent different manifestations of chi. They represent a classification system for everything in the universe, including people, some of these are shown in the "Relationships of the Five Elements" table.

Ideally, there should be a balance of all the elements. Where one dominates or is lacking, then difficulties occur. Interpreting and balancing the elements plays a major part in the practice of Feng Shui. The elements move in a predetermined way, illustrated as a cycle in which they all support each other. A useful way of remembering this is by looking at the cycle in the following way. Water enables Wood to grow, Wood enables Fire to burn resulting in ashes or Earth, in which forms Metal, which in liquid form resembles Water. Another cycle indicates how the elements control each other and can be memorized as follows: Water extinguishes Fire, and in turn is soaked up by the Earth, which is depleted of energy by Wood in the form of trees, which can be destroyed by Metal tools. the "Relationships of the Five Elements" table introduces another aspect – how in supporting another element, an element can itself be weakened. The applications of the five elements are illustrated throughout this book.

▲ *Storms are nature's way of restoring a balance. They replenish negative ions in the atmosphere, which improves air quality.*

▼ *The heavenly bodies are essential to our lives and their movements lie at the heart of Feng Shui.*

The Relationships of the Five Elements

Element	Helped by	Harmed by	Weakened by	Weakens
Wood	Water	Metal	Fire	Earth
Fire	Wood	Water	Earth	Metal
Earth	Fire	Wood	Metal	Water
Metal	Earth	Fire	Water	Wood
Water	Metal	Earth	Wood	Fire

The Five Elements

Element	Characteristics	Personalities	Associations
WOOD 	Symbolizes spring, growth and plant life. In its yin form, it is supple and pliable, in its yang form as sturdy as an oak. Positively used, it is a walking stick; negatively used, a spear. Bamboo is cherished in China for its ability to sway in the wind yet be used as scaffolding. Viewed as a tree, Wood energy is expansive, nurturing and versatile.	Wood people are public-spirited and energetic. Ideas people, their outgoing personalities win them support. They visualize rather than committing themselves to plans. *Positively* – they are artistic and undertake tasks with enthusiasm. *Negatively* – they become impatient and angry and often fail to finish the tasks they have begun.	Trees and plants Wooden furniture Paper Green Columns Decking Landscape pictures
FIRE 	Symbolizes summer, fire and heat. It can bring light, warmth and happiness or it can erupt, explode and destroy with great violence. Positively, it stands for honour and fairness. Negatively, it stands for aggression and war.	Fire people are leaders and crave action. They inspire others to follow, often into trouble, as they dislike rules and fail to see consequences. *Positively* – they are innovative, humorous and passionate people. *Negatively* – they are impatient, exploit others and have little thought for their feelings.	Sun symbols Candles, lights and lamps Triangles Red Man-made materials Sun or fire pictures
EARTH 	Symbolizes the nurturing environment that enables seeds to grow, from which all living things emanate and return to. It nurtures, supports and interacts with each of the other elements. Positively, it denotes fairness, wisdom and instinct. Negatively, it can smother or represent the nervous anticipation of non-existent problems.	Earth people are supportive and loyal. Practical and persevering, they are a tower of strength in a crisis. They do not rush anything, but their support is enduring. Patient and steady, they possess inner strength. *Positively* – earth people are loyal, dependable and patient. *Negatively* – they are obsessional and prone to nit-picking	Clay, brick and terracotta Cement and stone Squares Yellow, orange and brown
METAL 	Symbolizes autumn and strength. Its nature represents solidity and the ability to contain objects. On the other hand, metal is also a conductor. Positively, it represents communication, brilliant ideas and justice. Negatively, it can suggest destruction, danger and sadness. Metal can be a beautiful and precious commodity, or the blade of a weapon.	Metal people are dogmatic and resolute. They pursue their ambitious aims single-mindedly. Good organizers, they are independent and happy in their own company. Faith in their own abilities inclines them towards inflexibility although they thrive on change. They are serious and do not accept help easily. *Positively* – they are strong, intuitive and interesting people. *Negatively* – they are inflexible, melancholic and serious.	All metals Round shapes Domes Metal objects Door furniture and doorsteps Kitchenware White, grey, silver and gold Coins Clocks
WATER 	Symbolizes winter and water itself, gentle rain or a storm. It suggests the inner self, art and beauty. It touches everything. Positively, it nurtures and supports with understanding. Negatively, it can wear down and exhaust. Associated with the emotions, it can suggest fear, nervousness and stress.	Water people communicate well. They are diplomatic and persuasive. Sensitive to the moods of others, they will lend an ear. They are intuitive and make excellent negotiators. Flexible and adaptable, they view things holistically. *Positively* – water people are artistic, sociable and sympathetic. *Negatively* – water people are sensitive, fickle and intrusive.	Rivers, streams and lakes Blue and black Mirrors and glass Meandering patterns Fountains and ponds Fish tanks Water pictures

CHINESE ASTROLOGY

An analysis of an environment using a luo pan compass looks at the energetic qualities of the various compass points. The Earthly Branches represent 12 of these points and also correspond to the 12 animals which relate to Chinese astrology. We often find ourselves in situations at home, or at work, when we canot understand how another person can view the same situation so differently from us, or can make us feel uncomfortable, or find different things irritating or amusing. Looking at the animals enables us to explore these differences by allowing us an insight into the make-up of our natures and personalities.

With this knowledge, we can come to know ourselves better and to accept the personalities of others. At home, it may encourage us to think twice, for instance, before launching into a tirade on tidiness or punctuality. It also has an important use in the workplace in keeping warring factions apart and ensuring a harmonious balance between productive output and socializing.

The Cycles

The Chinese calendar is based on the cycle of the moon, which determines that each month is approximately 29½ days long, beginning with a new moon. The years progress in cycles of 12 and it is helpful to appreciate the subtleties of Chinese symbology since each year is represented by an animal and the characteristics of each animal and its way of life are used to identify different types of people. Cultural differences are apt to get in the way if we attempt this identification ourselves; whereas Westerners would describe the Rat's character, for example, as sly and crafty, the Chinese respect its quick mind and native cunning.

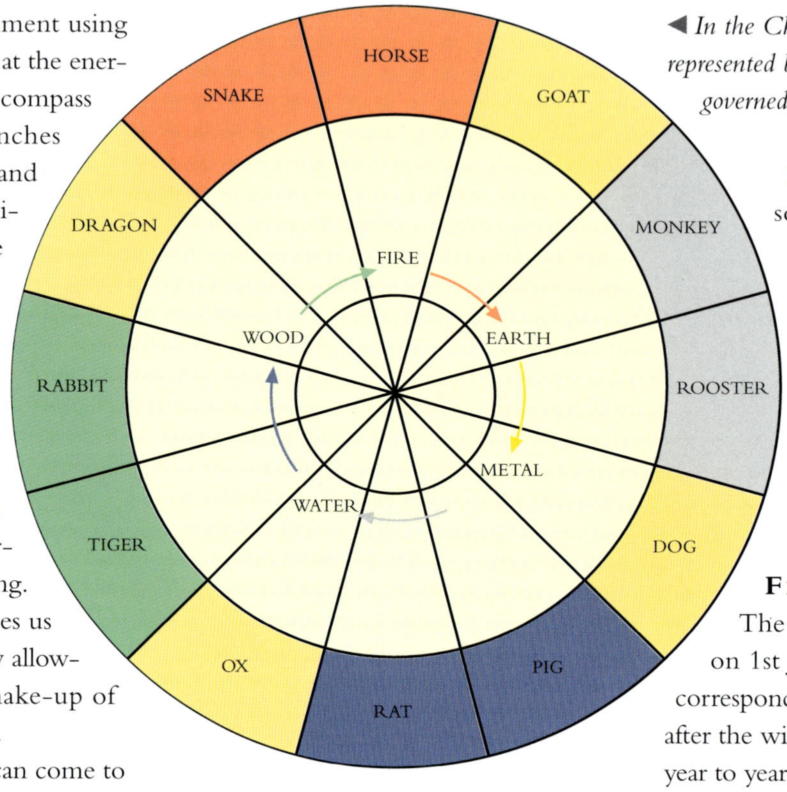

◀ *In the Chinese calendar each year is represented by an animal and each animal is governed by an element.*

Each animal is governed by an element which determines its intrinsic nature. The cycle of 12 is repeated five times to form a larger cycle of 60 years and in each of these cycles, the animals are ascribed an element with either a yin or yang characteristic, which determines their characters. Thus in 60 years, no two animals are the same. We begin by investigating the basic animal characteristics.

The Nature of the Animals

Animal	Element
Rat	Water
Ox	Earth
Tiger	Wood
Rabbit	Wood
Dragon	Earth
Snake	Fire
Horse	Fire
Goat	Earth
Monkey	Metal
Rooster	Metal
Dog	Earth
Pig	Water

If we do not get on with someone, it may be that the animals associated with us in the Chinese calendar are not compatible. Alternatively, it may be that the elements that represent the time of our birth are not in harmony with the elements of the other person.

Finding your Animal

The Chinese year does not begin on 1st January but on a date which corresponds with the second new moon after the winter equinox, so it varies from year to year. Thus someone born on 25th January 1960 according to the Western calendar would actually be born in 1959 according to the Chinese calendar. The "Chinese Animals Table" opposite gives the exact dates when each year begins and ends, as well as its ruling animal and element. Their outer characteristics are identified by the element of the year they were born, as shown in "The Nature of the Animals" box (left). The ways in which the elements affect an animal's personality are described in "The Five Elements" table.

Animal Cycles

The 12 animals represent each lunar month, each with its own element governing its intrinsic nature. Over 60 years, the Five Elements cycle spins so that each animal can be Wood, Fire, Earth, Metal or Water, which determines its character.

In a full analysis by an experienced Feng Shui consultant, each of us will have a collection of eight elements that together make up not only our characters, but also our destinies.

Chinese Animals Table

Year	Year Begins	Year Ends	Animal	Element
1920	20 February 1920	7 February 1921	Monkey	Metal +
1921	8 February 1921	27 January 1922	Rooster	Metal –
1922	28 January 1922	15 February 1923	Dog	Water +
1923	16 February 1923	4 February 1924	Pig	Water –
1924	5 February 1924	24 January 1925	Rat	Wood +
1925	25 January 1925	12 February 1926	Ox	Wood –
1926	13 February 1926	1 February 1927	Tiger	Fire +
1927	2 February 1927	22 January 1928	Rabbit	Fire –
1928	23 January 1928	9 February 1929	Dragon	Earth +
1929	10 February 1929	29 January 1930	Snake	Earth –
1930	30 January 1930	16 February 1931	Horse	Metal +
1931	17 February 1931	5 February 1932	Goat	Metal –
1932	6 February 1932	25 January 1933	Monkey	Water +
1933	26 January 1933	13 February 1934	Rooster	Water –
1934	14 February 1934	3 February 1935	Dog	Wood +
1935	4 February 1935	23 January 1936	Pig	Wood –
1936	24 January 1936	10 February 1937	Rat	Fire +
1937	11 February 1937	30 January 1938	Ox	Fire –
1938	31 January 1938	18 February 1939	Tiger	Earth +
1939	19 February 1939	7 February 1940	Rabbit	Earth –
1940	8 February 1940	26 January 1941	Dragon	Metal +
1941	27 January 1941	14 February 1942	Snake	Metal –
1942	15 February 1942	4 February 1943	Horse	Water +
1943	5 February 1943	24 January 1944	Goat	Water –
1944	25 January 1944	12 February 1945	Monkey	Wood +
1945	13 February 1945	1 February 1946	Rooster	Wood –
1946	2 February 1946	21 January 1947	Dog	Fire +
1947	22 January 1947	9 February 1948	Pig	Fire –
1948	10 February 1948	28 January 1949	Rat	Earth +
1949	29 January 1949	16 February 1950	Ox	Earth –
1950	17 February 1950	5 February 1951	Tiger	Metal +
1951	6 February 1951	26 January 1952	Rabbit	Metal –
1952	27 January 1952	13 February 1953	Dragon	Water +
1953	14 February 1953	2 February 1954	Snake	Water –
1954	3 February 1954	23 January 1955	Horse	Wood +
1955	24 January 1955	11 February 1956	Goat	Wood –
1956	12 February 1956	30 January 1957	Monkey	Fire +
1957	31 January 1957	17 February 1958	Rooster	Fire –
1958	18 February 1958	7 February 1959	Dog	Earth +
1959	8 February 1959	27 January 1960	Pig	Earth –
1960	28 January 1960	14 February 1961	Rat	Metal +
1961	15 February 1961	4 February 1962	Ox	Metal –
1962	5 February 1962	24 January 1963	Tiger	Water +
1963	25 January 1963	12 February 1964	Rabbit	Water –
1964	13 February 1964	1 February 1965	Dragon	Wood +
1965	2 February 1965	20 January 1966	Snake	Wood –
1966	21 January 1966	8 February 1967	Horse	Fire +
1967	9 February 1967	29 January 1968	Goat	Fire –
1968	30 January 1968	16 February 1969	Monkey	Earth +
1969	17 February 1969	5 February 1970	Rooster	Earth –
1970	6 February 1970	26 January 1971	Dog	Metal +
1971	27 January 1971	15 February 1972	Pig	Metal –
1972	16 February 1972	2 February 1973	Rat	Water +
1973	3 February 1973	22 January 1974	Ox	Water –
1974	23 January 1974	10 February 1975	Tiger	Wood +
1975	11 February 1975	30 January 1976	Rabbit	Wood –
1976	31 January 1976	17 February 1977	Dragon	Fire +
1977	18 February 1977	6 February 1978	Snake	Fire –
1978	7 February 1978	27 January 1979	Horse	Earth +
1979	28 January 1979	13 February 1980	Goat	Earth –
1980	14 February 1980	4 February 1981	Monkey	Metal +
1981	5 February 1981	24 January 1982	Rooster	Metal –
1982	25 January 1982	12 February 1983	Dog	Water +
1983	13 February 1983	1 February 1984	Pig	Water –
1984	2 February 1984	19 February 1985	Rat	Wood +
1985	20 February 1985	8 February 1986	Ox	Wood –
1986	9 February 1986	28 January 1987	Tiger	Fire +
1987	29 January 1987	16 February 1988	Rabbit	Fire –
1988	17 February 1988	5 February 1989	Dragon	Earth +
1989	6 February 1989	26 January 1990	Snake	Earth –
1990	27 January 1990	14 February 1991	Horse	Metal +
1991	15 February 1991	3 February 1992	Goat	Metal –
1992	4 February 1992	22 January 1993	Monkey	Water +
1993	23 January 1993	9 February 1994	Rooster	Water –
1994	10 February 1994	30 January 1995	Dog	Wood +
1995	31 January 1995	18 February 1996	Pig	Wood –
1996	19 February 1996	6 February 1997	Rat	Fire +
1997	7 February 1997	27 January 1998	Ox	Fire –
1998	28 January 1998	15 February 1999	Tiger	Earth +
1999	16 February 1999	4 February 2000	Rabbit	Earth –
2000	5 February 2000	23 January 2001	Dragon	Metal +
2001	24 January 2001	11 February 2002	Snake	Metal –
2002	12 February 2002	31 January 2003	Horse	Water +
2003	1 February 2003	21 January 2004	Goat	Water –
2004	22 January 2004	8 February 2005	Monkey	Wood +
2005	9 February 2005	28 January 2006	Rooster	Wood –
2006	29 January 2006	17 February 2007	Dog	Fire +
2007	18 February 2007	6 February 2008	Pig	Fire –
2008	7 February 2008	25 January 2009	Rat	Earth +
2009	26 January 2009	13 February 2010	Ox	Earth –
2010	14 February 2010	2 February 2011	Tiger	Metal +
2011	3 February 2011	22 January 2012	Rabbit	Metal –
2012	23 January 2012	9 February 2013	Dragon	Water +
2013	10 February 2013	30 January 2014	Snake	Water –

THE ANIMAL SIGNS

Using characteristics that are perceived to be an inherent part of the natures of the 12 animals, Chinese astrology attributes certain aspects of these to the characteristics and behaviour of people born at specific times. This system operates in much the same way as Western astrology.

The Rat

The Rat is an opportunist with an eye for a bargain. Rats tend to collect and hoard, but are unwilling to pay too much for anything. They are devoted to their families, particularly their children. On the surface, Rats are sociable and gregarious yet underneath they can be miserly and petty. Quick-witted and passionate, they are capable of deep emotions despite their cool exteriors. Their nervous energy and ambition may lead Rats to attempt more tasks than they are able to complete successfully. Rats will stand by their friends as long as they receive their support in return. However, they are not above using information given to them in confidence in order to advance their own cause.

鼠

▼ *Sociable and family-minded, rats are quick witted and opportunistic.*

▼ *Dependable and loyal, the Ox displays endless patience until pushed too far.*

▲ *Dynamic and generous, Tigers are warm-hearted unless they are crossed.*

The Ox

The Ox is solid and dependable. Oxen are excellent organizers and systematic in their approach to every task they undertake. They are not easily influenced by others' ideas. Loyalty is part of their make-up, but if crossed or deceived they will never forget. Oxen do not appear to be imaginative though they are capable of good ideas. Although not demonstrative or the most exciting people romantically, they are entirely dependable and make devoted parents. They are people of few words but fine understated gestures. Oxen are renowned for their patience, but it has its limits – once roused, their temper is a sight to behold.

牛

The Tiger

The Tiger is dynamic, impulsive and lives life to the full. Tigers often leap into projects without planning, but their natural exuberance will carry them through successfully unless boredom creeps in and they do not complete the task. Tigers do not like failure and need to be admired. If their spirits fall, they require a patient ear to listen until they bounce back again. They like excitement in their relationships and static situations leave them cold. Tigers are egotistic. They can be generous and warm, but will also sometimes show their claws.

虎

The Rabbit

兔

The Rabbit is a born diplomat and cannot bear conflict. Rabbits can be evasive and will often give the answer they think someone wishes to hear rather than enter into a discussion. This is not to say they give in easily: the docile cover hides a strong will and self-assurance. It is difficult to gauge what Rabbits are thinking and they can often appear to be constantly daydreaming, though in reality they may be planning their next strategy. The calmest of the animal signs, Rabbits are social creatures up to the point when their space is invaded. Good communication skills enable Rabbits to enjoy the company of others and they are good counsellors. They prefer to keep away from the limelight where possible and to enjoy the finer things of life.

▲ *Good counsellors and communicators, Rabbits also need their own space.*

The Dragon

The Dragon will launch straight into projects or conversations with a pioneering spirit. Dragons often fail to notice others trying to keep up or indeed those plotting behind their backs. Authority figures, they make their own laws and cannot bear restriction. They prefer to get on with a job themselves and are good at motivating others into action.

▲ *Powerful leaders, Dragons prefer to follow their own path in life.*

龍

They are always available to help others, but their pride makes it difficult for them to accept help in return. Although they are always at the centre of things, they tend to be loners and are prone to stress when life becomes difficult. Hard-working and generous, Dragons are entirely trustworthy and are loyal friends. They enjoy excitement and new situations. When upset, they can be explosive, but all is soon forgotten.

The Snake

The Snake is a connoisseur of the good things in life. Inward-looking and self-reliant, Snakes tend to keep their own counsel and dislike relying on others. They can be ruthless in pursuing their goals. Although very kind and generous, Snakes can be demanding in relationships. They find it hard to forgive and will never forget a slight. Never underestimate the patience of a snake, who will wait in the wings until the time is right to strike. They are elegant and sophisticated and although they are good at making money, they never spend it on trifles. Only the best is good enough for them. Very intuitive, Snakes can sense the motives of others and can sum up situations accurately. If crossed, Snakes will bite back with deadly accuracy. They exude an air of mystery, ooze charm and can be deeply passionate.

▼ *Mysterious and passionate, Snakes have endless patience.*

▲ *Active and excitable, the Horse's nervous energy often runs away with them.*

The Horse

馬

The Horse is ever-active. Horses will work tirelessly until a project is completed, but only if the deadline is their own. Horses have lightning minds and can sum up people and situations in an instant, sometimes too quickly, and they will move on before seeing the whole picture. Capable of undertaking several tasks at once, Horses are constantly on the move and fond of exercise. They may exhaust themselves physically and mentally. Horses are ambitious and confident in their own abilities. They are not interested in the opinions of others and are adept at side-stepping issues. They can be impatient and have explosive tempers although they rarely bear grudges.

The Goat

羊

The Goat is emotional and compassionate. Peace-lovers, Goats always behave correctly and they are extremely accommodating to others. They tend to be shy and vulnerable to criticism. They worry a lot and appear to be easily put upon, but when they feel strongly about something they will dig their heels in and sulk until they achieve their objectives. Goats are generally popular and are usually well cared for by others. They appreciate the finer things in life and are usually lucky. They find it difficult to deal with difficulties and deprivation. Ardent romantics, Goats can obtain their own way by wearing their partners down and turning every occasion to their advantage. They will do anything to avoid conflict and hate making decisions.

▼ *Peace-loving Goats are kind and popular, they hate conflict and will try to avoid it.*

The Monkey

猴

The Monkey is intelligent and capable of using its wits to solve problems. Monkeys often wriggle out of difficult situations and are not above trickery if it will further their own ends. Monkeys tend to be oblivious of other people and of the effect their own actions may have on them. In spite of this, they are usually popular and are able to motivate others by their sheer enthusiasm for new projects. Monkeys are constantly on the look out for new challenges and their innovative approach and excellent memories generally make them successful. They are full of energy and are always active. They have little sympathy for those who are unable to keep up with them, but will soon forget any difficulties.

▼ *Energetic Monkeys use their intelligence to push their own ideas forward.*

▲ *The flamboyant Rooster can be easily won over by flattery and admiration.*

The Rooster

雞

The Rooster is a very sociable creature. Roosters shine in situations where they are able to be the centre of attention. If a Rooster is present, everyone will be aware of the fact because no Rooster can ever take a back seat at a social gathering. They are dignified, confident and extremely strong-willed, yet they may have a negative streak. They excel in arguments and debates. Incapable of underhandedness, Roosters lay all their cards on the table and do not spare others' feelings in their quest to do the right thing. They never weary of getting to the bottom of a problem and are perfectionists in all that they do. Roosters can usually be won over by flattery. Full of energy, Roosters are brave, but they hate criticism and can be puritanical in their approach to life.

The Dog

犬

The Dog is entirely dependable and has an inherent sense of justice. Intelligent, Dogs are loyal to their friends and they always listen to the problems of others, although they can be critical. In a crisis, Dogs will always help and they will never betray a friend. They can be hard workers, but are not all that interested in accumulating wealth for themselves. They like to spend time relaxing. Dogs take time to get to know people but have a tendency to pigeon-hole them. When they want something badly they can be persistent. If roused they can be obstinate and occasionally they lash out, although their temper is usually short-lived. Some Dogs can be rather nervous and they may be prone to pessimism.

▼ *Dogs are loyal and hard-working, but enjoy relaxing too.*

▲ *Peace-loving Pigs are sociable and popular and are able to organize others well.*

The Pig

豬

The Pig is everybody's friend. Honest and generous, Pigs are always available to bail others out of difficulties. Pigs love the social scene and are popular. They rarely argue and if they do fly off the handle, they bear no grudges afterwards. They abhor conflict and very often will not notice when others are attempting to upset them. They prefer to think well of people. Over-indulgence is their greatest weakness and Pigs will spend heavily in pursuit of pleasure. They always share with their friends and trust that, in return, their friends will make allowances for their own little weaknesses. Great organizers, Pigs like to have a cause and will often rally others to it as well.

COMPATIBILITY OF SIGNS

The saying, "You can choose your friends but not your family", is often heard from those who do not have harmonious family relationships, and we all find that we are drawn more to some people than to others. Chinese astrology uses the year, month, day and time of birth (each of which is represented by an animal and the yin or yang attributes of its accompanying element) to analyse characters and predict fortunes. Analyses of relationships depend upon the interaction of the elements on each person's chart. We can gain some insight into our own characters and those of our family and colleagues by using the "Chinese Animals Table" and then looking at the associated elements with their yang (+) (positive characteristics) or yin (–) (negative characteristics) in "The Five Elements" table.

▲ *We function well at work when we are compatible with our colleagues. The man on the right looks uncomfortable.*

▼ *We are drawn to people for a variety of reasons. Compatibility of animal signs and elements can certainly help.*

▼ *This table shows which of our family, friends and colleagues we relate to best according to Chinese astrology.*

COMPATIBILITY TABLE

	RAT	OX	TIGER	RABBIT	DRAGON	SNAKE	HORSE	GOAT	MONKEY	ROOSTER	DOG	PIG
RAT	+	=	+	–	★	=	–	–	★	–	+	+
OX	=	+	–	=	+	★	–	–	+	★	–	+
TIGER	+	–	+	–	+	–	★	+	–	=	★	=
RABBIT	+	+	–	+	=	+	–	★	–	–	=	★
DRAGON	★	–	+	=	–	+	–	+	★	+	–	=
SNAKE	+	★	–	+	=	+	–	=	–	★	+	–
HORSE	–	–	★	–	=	+	–	=	+	+	★	+
GOAT	–	–	=	★	+	+	=	+	+	–	–	★
MONKEY	★	+	–	–	★	–	–	+	=	+	+	=
ROOSTER	–	★	+	–	=	★	+	=	–	–	+	+
DOG	+	–	★	=	–	+	★	–	+	–	=	+
PIG	=	+	=	★	+	–	–	★	–	+	+	–

KEY: ★ Excellent = Good + Workable – Difficult

THE ANIMAL YEARS

As we have seen, each year is ruled by an animal and its character is said to denote the energetic quality of the year.

The animal which rules each year and the date of the Chinese New Year for around a hundred-year period are shown on the "Chinese Animals Table". For ease of reference, 1999–2010 are shown below. Our fortunes in each year are indicated by whether or not we are compatible with the animal ruling that year, which can be checked by referring back to the "Compatibility Table".

1999	Rabbit	2005	Rooster
2000	Dragon	2006	Dog
2001	Snake	2007	Pig
2002	Horse	2008	Rat
2003	Goat	2009	Ox
2004	Monkey	2010	Tiger

Year of the Rabbit

A respite from the past year and a breather before the next, rest is indicated here. This is a time for negotiations and settlements, but not for new ventures. Women's and family concerns are considered important.

Year of the Dragon

The time for new business ventures and projects. Euphoric and unpredictable, this is the year for outlandish schemes and taking risks. Dragon babies are considered lucky.

Year of the Snake

Peace returns and allows time to reflect. Care should be taken in business matters as treachery and underhand dealings are indicated. Money is made and communication is good. A fertile year, in which morality becomes an issue.

Year of the Horse

An energetic and volatile year in which money will be spent and borrowed. Some impulsive behaviour will bring rewards, while some will fail. A year for marriage and divorce.

Year of the Goat

A quiet year in which family matters are to the fore. A year for consolidating and for diplomatic negotiations, rather than launching new projects.

Year of the Monkey

An unpredictable year when nothing goes according to plan. Only the quick-witted will prosper. New ideas abound and communication will flourish.

Year of the Rooster

A year for making feelings known and letting grievances out. This may cause disharmony in families so tact is required.

Year of the Dog

Worthy causes abound – human and animal rights and environmental issues are in the public eye. Security should be checked, by governments and at home. A year for marriage and the family.

Year of the Pig

The last year of the cycle and unfinished business should be concluded. Optimism abounds and the pursuit of leisure is indicated. Family concerns will go well.

Year of the Rat

This is a lucky year, a good time to start a new venture. The rewards will not come without hard work, but with careful planning they will arrive.

Year of the Ox

Harvest is the symbol for this year so we will reap what we have sown. Decisions should be made now and contracts signed. This is a conservative year so grand or outrageous schemes are not considered appropriate.

Year of the Tiger

Sudden conflicts and crises arise in this year and will have an impact for some time. The year for grand schemes for the courageous, but underhand activities may suffer from repercussions.

▼ *Family relationships are usually harmonious if the animal signs are compatible and the elements do not clash.*

THE BAGUA AND THE MAGIC SQUARE

The compass directions and their associations are fundamental to the practice of Feng Shui. Astronomical and geomantic calculations and the place of human beings within them are plotted on a luo pan, an instrument so powerful that it has been likened to a computer. The luo pan can indicate, to those who know how to interpret it, which illness someone in a certain location might be suffering from, or the fortunes of a person living in a certain room in a house.

This vast amount of information has been reduced to a shorthand form incorporated in a "Magic Square". In cultures worldwide, this was used as a talisman. Many formulae based on the magic square are used to discover whether a place is auspicious, in itself and for the people living there, and the simplest of these are introduced in this book. The diagram on the right shows how the energies represented by the Magic Square always move in a fixed pattern. These patterns are repeated over time and can indicate the fortunes of a person or building in a certain year.

THE BAGUA

The information contained in the luo pan is condensed into the magic square, which forms the basis of the Bagua, or Pa Kua, a tool we can use to investigate our homes and offices. The Bagua below holds some of the images which describe the energies of the eight directions and the central position. The Bagua represents the journey of life, the Tao, and we can use it to create comfortable living, working and leisure spaces.

When applying Feng Shui principles to your house, garden or office you will need a tracing of the Bagua with the colours,compass points and directions all added on.

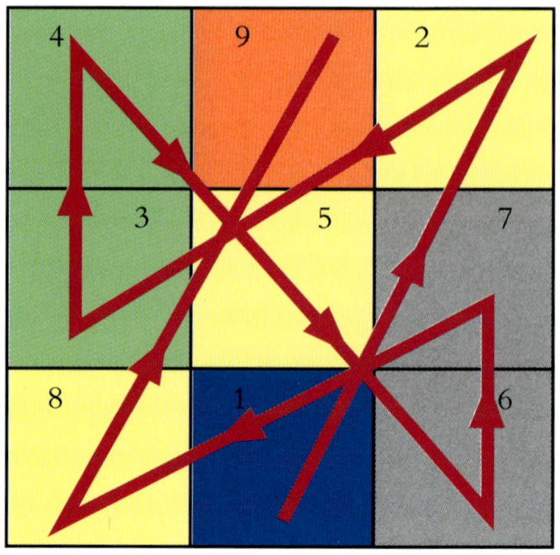

▲ *The Magic Square: the "magic" lies in the fact that every line adds up to 15. Magic squares exist all over the world. In ancient cultures, such symbols were a source of power to their initiates. In Hebrew culture, the pattern formed by the movement of energies is known as the seal of Saturn and is used in Western magic. In Islamic cultures, intricate patterns are based on complex magic squares.*

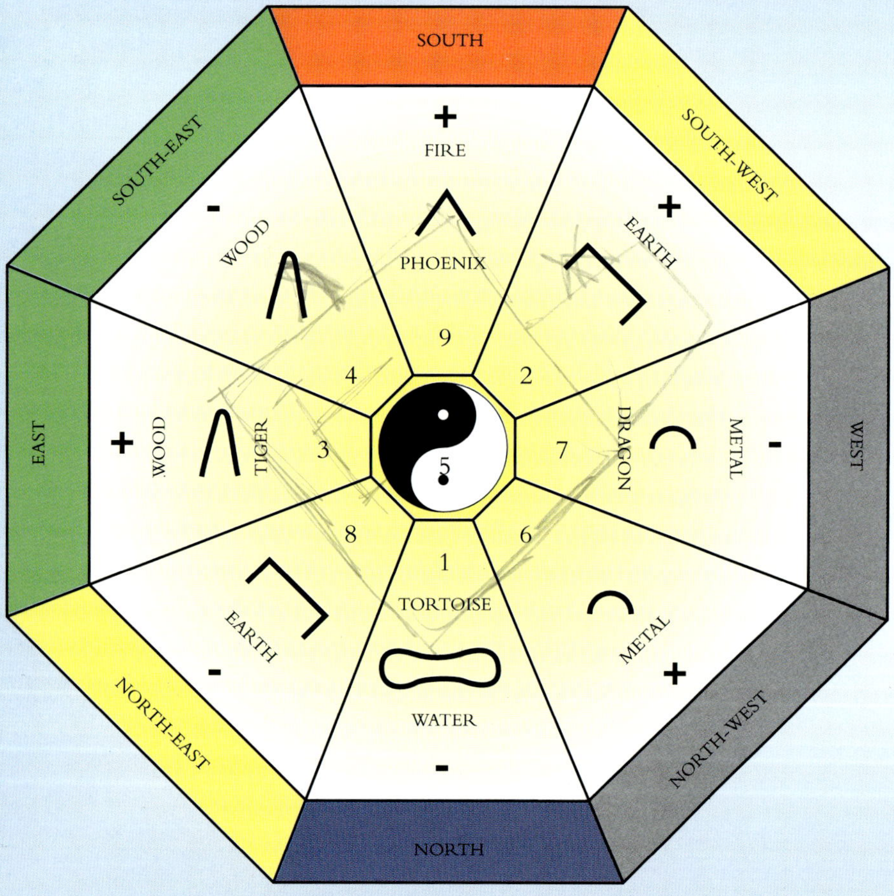

THE BAGUA, OR PA KUA

This diagram shows the energies associated with each of the eight directions. The outer bar shows the colours and directions associated with the five elements. The symbolds indicate the yin (-) or yang (+) quality of the element associated with each direction. Also shown are the shapes associated with each element. The four symbolic animals which represent the energy of each of the four cardinal directions – north, south, east, west are indicated, and the numbers of the Magic Square are shown in their associated directions. We take on the characteristics of a number and the energies associated with it, which are thought to shape who we are, where we feel comfortable, and our fortunes. The Chinese compass is always drawn facing south since this is the favoured direction for houses to face in parts of China. This does not affect the actual magnetic north-south directions.

FINDING YOUR MAGIC NUMBER

To complete the picture, it is necessary to discover how human beings fit into the scheme. Each person is allocated a "magic" number that enables them to position themselves to their best advantage. Before finding our number from the tables opposite, we must check the date of the Chinese New Year from the "Chinese Animals Table". The previous year is used if our birthday falls before the start of the new year.

▼ *Each of the magic numbers represents a particular type of energy suggested by the annual nature cycle. Find your number on the table and discover your energy below.*

Energy of Numbers

1: Water. Winter. Independent. Intuitive
2: Earth. Late Summer. Methodical.
3: Thunder. Spring. Progressive
4: Wind. Late Spring. Adaptable.
5: Earth. Central Force. Assertive.
6: Heaven. Late Autumn. Unyielding.
7: Lake. Autumn. Flexible. Nervous.
8: Mountain. Late Winter. Obstinate. Energetic.
9. Fire. Summer. Impulsive. Intelligent.

Using the Magic Numbers

Some Feng Shui consultants use only the male, or yang, numbers in their calculations, some use both male and female, or yin, numbers. Others regard the yin (female) numbers as depicting the inner self, while the yang (male) numbers represent the image a person presents to the world. Traditional male and female stereotypes are no longer the norm. Modern men and women, with more interchangeable roles, tend to have both yin and yang characteristics.

East-west Directions

People tend to fare better in some directions than in others. They fall into two groups, the east group or the west group. Those who fall into the east group should live in a house facing an east group direction, those in the west group a west group direction. If this is not possible, your bed and/or your chair should face an appropriate direction.

▼ *Once you have found your magic number, you can identify which group you are in, east or west, which directions suit you. and whether your house is compatible.*

Group	Numbers	Directions
East	1, 3, 4, 9	N, E, SE, S
West	2, 5, 6, 7, 8	SW, NW, W, NE, CENTRE

The Magic Numbers

YEAR	M	F	YEAR	M	F	YEAR	M	F	YEAR	M	F
1920	8	7	1952	3	3	1984	7	8	2002	7	8
1921	7	8	1953	2	4	1985	6	9	2003	6	9
1922	6	9	1954	1	5	1986	5	1	2004	5	1
1923	5	1	1955	9	6	1987	4	2	2005	4	2
1924	4	2	1956	8	7	1988	3	3	2006	3	3
1925	3	3	1957	7	8	1989	2	4	2007	2	4
1926	2	4	1958	6	9	1990	1	5	2008	1	5
1927	1	5	1959	5	1	1991	9	6	2009	9	6
1928	9	6	1960	4	2	1992	8	7	2010	8	7
1929	8	7	1961	3	3	1993	7	8	2011	7	8
1930	7	8	1962	2	4	1994	6	9	2012	6	9
1931	6	9	1963	1	5	1995	5	1	2013	5	1
1932	5	1	1964	9	6	1996	4	2	2014	4	2
1933	4	2	1965	8	7	1997	3	3	2015	3	3
1934	3	3	1966	7	8	1998	2	4	2016	2	4
1935	2	4	1967	6	9	1999	1	5	2017	1	5
1936	1	5	1968	5	1	2000	9	6	2018	9	6
1937	9	6	1969	4	2	2001	8	7	2019	8	7
1938	8	7	1970	3	3						
1939	7	8	1971	2	4						
1940	6	9	1972	1	5						
1941	5	1	1973	9	6						
1942	4	2	1974	8	7						
1943	3	3	1975	7	8						
1944	2	4	1976	6	9						
1945	1	5	1977	5	1						
1946	9	6	1978	4	2						
1947	8	7	1979	3	3						
1948	7	8	1980	2	4						
1949	6	9	1981	1	5						
1950	5	1	1982	9	6						
1951	4	2	1983	8	7						

Key: M = male F = female

▼ *A Chinese Feng Shui expert studies the luo pan (compass).*

PERCEPTION AND THE SYMBOLIC BAGUA

Much of the skill in undertaking a Feng Shui survey of our immediate environment is in reading the signals there. If we are healthy and happy, this may prove to be a comparatively easy process. If we are not, our perception may be coloured by our emotional or physical state and we may not be able to see things clearly.

The Chinese phrase "First, luck; second, destiny; third, Feng Shui; fourth, virtues; fifth, education" is worth repeating, as it shows that to some extent our fortunes and personalities are out of our hands. If we embrace Feng Shui, think and act positively, and make use of the knowledge the universe has to offer, then we can begin to take charge of the parts of our lives that we can control and make the best of them.

Part of the process of Feng Shui is to awaken our senses and sensibilities to our environment. Among other things, each of the Five Elements governs different senses, and our aim is to create a balanced environment in which all our senses are satisfied and none is allowed to predominate over the rest to create an imbalance.

We can heighten our perception of the world if we introduce ourselves to different experiences. Take an objective look at your weekly routine and decide on a new experience or activity which will add something different to your life.

A Magical Template

When Feng Shui began to take off in the West several years ago, the workings of the compass were known only to a handful of scholars. Those early days were distinguished by the creation of, and endless discussions on, the workings of the Bagua. It was used then, as it is now, by the Tibetan Black Hat practitioners, as a magical template that is aligned with a front door, the entrance to a room, the front of a desk or even a face.

This template is then used to supply information which can enable us to understand our energy and make corrections to create balance and harmony. Some Chinese practitioners have since

A Healthy Lifestyle and a Healthy Mind

Stuck energy in our homes is often a reflection of our lifestyle and state of mind. A healthy daily regime will make us receptive to the powers of Feng Shui.

Ideally, we should take time out each day to meditate – or just to escape from stress. Often a short walk, gardening or a few minutes sitting quietly will help us to relax. Holidays and new experiences can help our mental energy.

Chi Kung and T'ai Chi are part of the same system. Their exercise programmes help to keep the energy channels in the body unblocked, while also releasing the mind.

Eating a healthy balanced diet of food-stuffs, produced without chemical interference, is another way of ensuring that harmful energies, or toxins, do not upset our bodily balance.

If we do become ill, acupuncture and acupressure and Chinese herbal medicine can balance the energies in our bodies and help to keep us fit.

◀ *Meditation (left), hiking in the mountains (bottom left) or a daily session of T'ai Chi (bottom right) will all benefit our mental energy and help to heighten our perceptions.*

▲ *Mountains afford protection to the rear and sides of this village, while a lake in front accumulates chi – all that remains is to arrange the inside of the house to create a supportive environment.*

sought to use the Bagua alongside the compass method. They place it over the plan of a home so that it is positioned with the Career area in the north, irrespective of where the front door lies.

Other traditional Chinese approaches concentrate on interpreting the energies indicated by the Five Elements and by the rings of the luo pan. Such is the "magic" of Feng Shui that, in the right hands, all approaches appear to work.

Newcomers to Feng Shui may find it difficult to connect to a compass. Hopefully, they will use either method to experience for themselves the magic of the early days of discovery, and will be drawn deeper into this amazing philosophy, gaining an insight into its power.

▼ *The Three Gates Bagua. This may be entered through "Career" (back), "Knowledge" (bottom left) or "Helpful People" (bottom right). The compass Bagua with associated colours and shapes is shown inside to help you balance the elements of your home.*

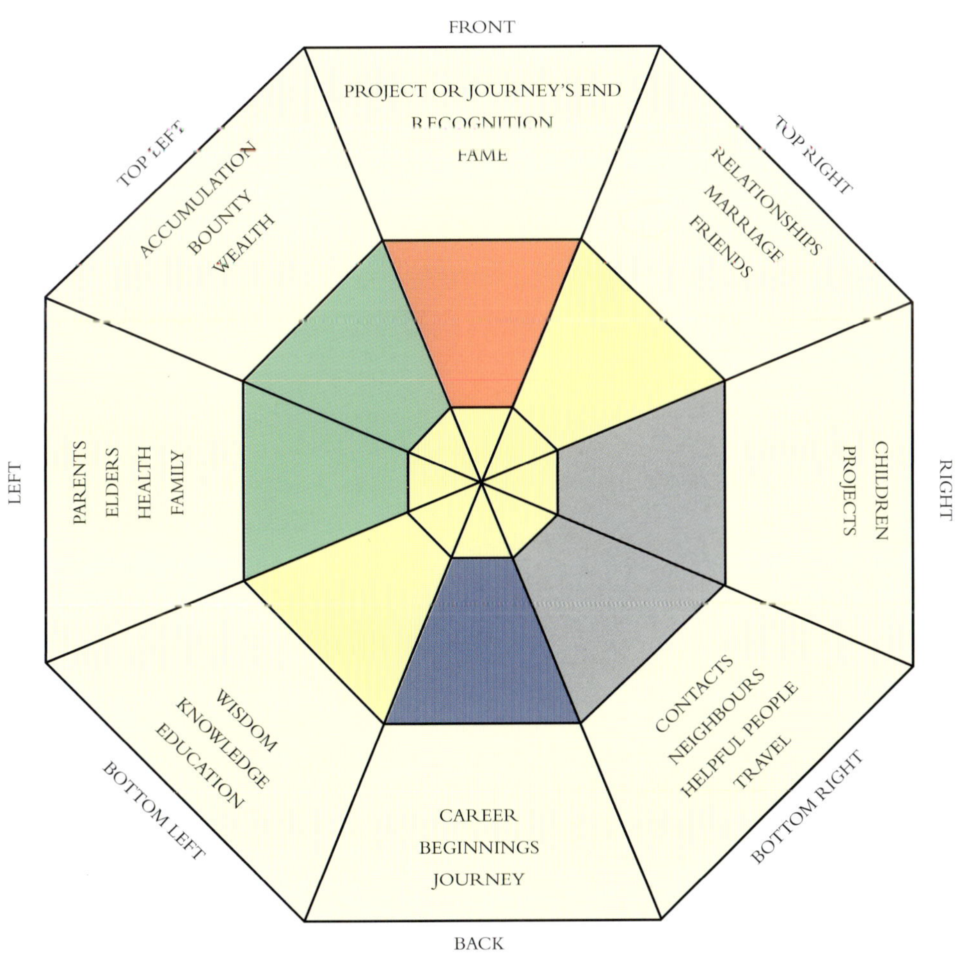

The Symbolic Bagua

Throughout this book we will see how various images are connected to each of the eight points of the Magic Square or the Bagua, which is based on it. The symbolic Bagua uses the energies of each direction to relate to the journey of life. The journey begins at the entrance to our home – the mouth of chi – and moves in a predetermined way through the home until it reaches its conclusion. By focusing on an aspect of our lives which we want to stimulate or change, we can use the energies of the universe and make them work for us. Psychologically, focusing on an area enables us to create the circumstances to bring about change.

So far, a traditional compass approach has been used, but the diagram to the left allows us to use either approach. From now on readers should feel free to connect with the Bagua as they wish, and through it to the intangible forces which make this such a fascinating subject. Most people who have used Feng Shui have experienced changes in their circumstances. These often correspond to the actual energy around a relationship or situation rather than our desires. The results will ultimately serve our best interests, but the outcome is often unexpected.

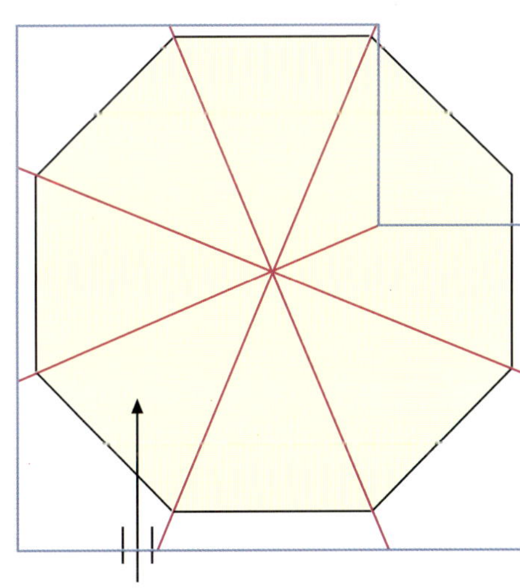

▲ *The Three Gates Bagua is flexible. If a home has an irregular shape, the corresponding area of the Bagua is also considered to be missing. In this house, the front entrance is in the "Knowledge" area and the "Relationships" part of the house is missing.*

FENG SHUI IN THE MODERN WORLD

Modern lifestyles are far removed from those of our ancestors. For them, charting the progress of the moon and sun, and interpreting the different weather conditions and other activities occurring in the natural world in relation to the movement of the stars and planets was essential, since they depended on the land to provide them with the means to survive. The modern city-dweller may never see food growing naturally and may not even be able to view the night sky because of pollution and neon lighting. However, we still depend on the natural world for our well-being. We can be at the mercy of hurricanes, or bask on sun-drenched beaches; mountains may erupt, or provide sustenance for livestock; human beings can pollute the air and contaminate the land, or create sanctuaries for wildlife species.

▲ *Nighttime in Mexico City. The 23 million inhabitants are denied a view of the stars because of neon lighting and pollution.*

▶ *The rice harvest in traditional regions of China has used many of the same processes for the past thousand years.*

▼ *There are still thriving cultures in which ancient skills and lifestyles remain such as this village in Chad.*

Ancient peoples, through necessity, regarded the heavens, the earth and themselves as part of one system. This holistic view of life has persisted in many cultures, where health and medicine, food and lifestyle are all interconnected. In the West, scientific development created different disciplines which advanced in isolation from each other. Through recent movements in health and food production, we are seeking to correct the imbalances caused by this approach. The Tao, or the Way, the philosophy which underlies Feng Shui, shows how it is possible to order our lives to exist in harmony with each other and the natural world. We can use Feng Shui to help us work towards achieving this.

The traditional concept of Gaia, the Greek earth goddess, was used by James Lovelock and Lynne Margulis in the 1970s to encourage us to perceive the world as a biosphere in which each constituent part has a role to play. In order to understand Feng Shui we need to expand this concept of ecosystems further to include human beings and the impact of

▲ *In 1948 science writer Fred Hoyle predicted: "Once a photograph of the Earth taken from the outside world is available … a new idea as powerful as any other in history will be let loose." The environmental awareness movement began at the time human beings landed on the moon.*

the cosmos, and to expand our awareness so that we can predict the consequences of our actions.

As we investigate the ideas behind Feng Shui and consider practical ways of introducing them into our lives, we also need to shift our perception. Feng Shui in the modern world incorporates intuition. Maori warriors navigate hundreds of miles by the feel of a place and by observing signs. The Inuit language incorporates many words to describe the complexities of different types of snow. Similarly, we can heighten our awareness of our environment by adopting the principles of Feng Shui.

Until recently navigators used the stars to steer by, and in some parts of the world those who work with the land still use the stars to determine planting times for their crops. These people recognize patterns in the interrelationship between different parts of the natural world, noticing which plants are in flower or when birds return from migration and comparing them to the weather. Many customs are firmly based in natural wisdom.

Working with the Natural World

A good example of working with the natural world is provided by an apparently admirable scheme to plant 300 oak forests in Britain to celebrate the millennium. But in the natural world oak trees grow singly and not in rows in large groups, and recent research has indicated that where many oaks grow together there is a higher incidence of Lyme disease, a debilitating illness which attacks the nervous system. The reason for this is that mice and deer feed on acorns and also carry the ticks which transmit the disease. Thus, where there are many oaks, there is also a high incidence of Lyme disease. Mixed planting, which mirrors the natural world, would be preferable.

In order to save money, one forest was planted with Polish oak trees that came into bud two weeks later than the native trees. This meant there were no caterpillars feeding on the buds to provide food for newly-hatched fledglings. These mistakes might have been avoided if Taoistic principles had been applied to the scheme.

▼ *Native trees act as the Tortoise, Dragon, Tiger formation to protect these buildings.*

犬

雞

鼠

龍

猴

THE FENG SHUI GARDEN

THE ORIGINS OF FENG SHUI LIE IN AN ANCIENT CIVILIZATION WHICH GREW THEIR CROPS BY TAPPING INTO THE BENEFICIAL ENERGIES AROUND THEM. GARDENS OFFER US THE SAME OPPORTUNITY TO CONNECT TO THE NATURAL WORLD, AND THE UNIVERSE BEYOND. IN THE GARDEN WE ARE IN PARTNERSHIP WITH OTHER LIVING THINGS. IF WE WORK WITH THEM, BALANCE AND HARMONY WILL FOLLOW.

豬

INTRODUCTION

When we purchase a house or move into an apartment our first concerns are likely to be the number of bedrooms, the size of the kitchen and the condition of the roof. Rarely do we choose a home on the basis of its garden, even though it can play an important role in correcting the imbalance created by the frantic pace of modern living. We are driven in pursuit of work and its rewards, bombarded with stimulating experiences via the media, and we can even shop 24 hours a day if we want to. These yang activities take their toll on our mental and physical health. An excellent way to redress the balance is to create quiet havens for ourselves in our gardens.

When we recall the books we read as children, many of our favourite stories were set in the countryside. There can be few of us who have not, at some point in our lives, peered into a hole in search of Brer Rabbit or walked by a river hoping to see Ratty and Mole or Mr Toad sweeping by in his magnificent car. The magic of raindrops on a spider's web, the first ladybird to land on a small pudgy finger, a beautiful mahogany-coloured chestnut and the swish of autumn leaves as we wade through in shiny boots, these are all early experiences which link us to the natural world.

▲ *However small, a garden can offer us a retreat from the hurly-burly of modern life.*

▶ *Studying details such as a spider's web enables us to make links with nature.*

▼ *Green spaces in the inner city give the inhabitants a relief from stress.*

Until quite recently, gardens for contemplation were the preserve of the rich. Poorer people cultivated the soil for their survival, but their hard work did keep them in touch with the land. There are many children now who have never seen fruit or vegetables growing or experienced the magic of watching a tiny seed develop into a plant. Our gardens are furnished like our homes with everything bought off-the-peg from garden centres. But the mood is changing. In big cities like London and New York there are moves to create community gardens on derelict sites between inner-city buildings and skyscrapers. More and more schools are creating gardens to teach children about the natural world. The demand for food uncontaminated by chemicals is growing as we begin to realize the folly of some of the current trends in industrial food production. It seems that there is a latent longing to reconnect with the natural world.

In the Feng Shui garden the design principles of the ancient Chinese landscapers are used to create, not Chinese gardens, but indigenous ones which relate to our own psyche as well as to the spirit of the place where we live. By using local plants and natural methods to grow them we can make a garden in which we can distance ourselves from the hurly-burly of modern living and gain repose. Even if we live in an apartment block, we can take the initiative by tending the ill-kept communal spaces which provide our window to the outside world. We need to have restful yet energizing green spaces when we return to the nurturing space of our home.

▲ *Choose plants to suit the soil and situation for a healthy, harmonious garden.*

▼ *With some pots, seeds and imagination, we can create tranquil and beautiful spaces.*

The following pages reveal how the ancient principles of Feng Shui can be employed in our gardens today to create supportive and nurturing environments. We will see how centuries-old formulae can be translated into modern-day garden design techniques and discover how yin and yang and the Five Elements can be interpreted outside.

Feng Shui is the art of directing the energy of an environment to move in ways with which we feel comfortable. The plants, furnishings and other objects we surround ourselves with have an impact on how we feel about the garden and how we use it. The ever-present unseen energies of the earth and the universe can be exploited to our advantage.

FENG SHUI PRINCIPLES IN THE GARDEN

Taoist principles lie at the heart of Chinese garden design and can be seen in the ancient gardens in the province of Suzhou today. Many of the principles are echoed in what is considered to be good garden design around the world. Other principles stem from the culture and mythology of China and are not included here, since every culture has its own beliefs and practices which are part of its heritage and should be preserved. Feng Shui allows for these differences. Hopefully, with an adaptation of the principles we will be able to develop our own gardens in a way which will enhance our lives.

CHINESE GARDENS

Chinese gardens originated in the centres of power, the homes of the wealthy and around religious sites, and they represent an attempt to recreate the perfection of nature and the unity of human beings, Heaven and Earth. In China, garden design conforms to the same philosophical principles as the other arts. It grew out of the fusion of the Confucian concept of art, as something created by human beings but modelled on nature, and the Taoist belief in the superiority of the natural world as an art form. It produced some of the most dramatic yet tranquil places in the world.

In China, the garden and home are considered to be a single entity. The garden is drawn into the house through windows and latticed panels, while the walls serve as backdrops to carefully chosen plants. Chinese gardens are designed to accommodate human beings and their activities so buildings are a major feature, whether for recreation, as viewing platforms, or as observatories. In the same way that European landscape architects like "Capability" Brown and Humphrey Repton used the natural scenery as a backdrop to their gardens, ancient Chinese designers incorporated mountains, natural water features and trees into theirs. If such natural features were absent they created them, building hills and importing large rocks to emulate mountains. It was said that the Sung Dynasty fell because the Emperor became obsessed with transporting huge rocks for his garden from a remote province and bankrupted the state.

Chinese domestic architecture determined a key concept of garden design. Houses were built around three sides of a central courtyard, and the empty centre is an important feature of Feng Shui. Whereas Western designers might fill the

▲ *Large gnarled rocks are used in Chinese gardens to symbolize mountains, and are often subjects of meditation.*

▼ *Mountains and water – shan shui – are essential features of the gardens of China.*

▼ *This garden in England shows natural planting typical of Chinese-style gardens.*

▲ *Open, enclosed and covered spaces all feature in the design of the Chinese garden.*

PLANTS AND THEIR MEANINGS

Aspidistra: Fortitude
Chrysanthemum: Resolution
Cypress: Nobility
Gardenia: Strength
Hydrangea: Achievement
Kerria: Individualism
Orchid: Endurance
Peony: Wealth
Pine: Longevity
Pomegranate: Fertility
Rhododendron: Delicacy
Virginia Creeper: Tenacity

centres of enclosed spaces with geometrically aligned beds, the Taoist view of a space lies in its potential. It is not a lifeless void, but an energetic area brimming with possibilities. Walls are given meaning by inserting windows which look to the world beyond, rocks are brought to life by the hollows and crevices which give them character.

According to the Tao, human activity should never dictate the shape of the natural world, since all things should be allowed to develop naturally. Thus the clipped trees and hedges which can be seen in Western gardens do not occur in a Chinese garden where the natural forms of trees are allowed to develop. Whatever alterations are carried out in a Chinese garden, the result must look natural. Ponds, lakes and hills all resemble their natural counterparts.

The aesthetic principles behind all Chinese art forms, as well as the moral and ethical principles on which society is built, are all based on observations and interpretations of the natural world. Human characteristics are compared with natural phenomena, such as stone, bamboo and blossoms. Mountains and water, which play an integral part in the study of Feng Shui, feature largely in Chinese gardens and paintings.

▶ *Openings in walls and windows offer inviting glimpses of pleasures to come.*

▲ *According to Taoist principles, the interest of these stones lies in their holes, since it is they that bring the stones to life.*

▶ *The design of this garden is based on natural plant forms, rocks and water.*

THE FENG SHUI GARDEN

▲ *Observations of the natural world and an understanding of the laws of nature led to the creation of the formulae on which Feng Shui is based.*

The "Magic Square" on which Feng Shui is based represents a picture of the universe. Its arrangement lies at the heart of Feng Shui and represents the dynamic interaction of all natural phenomena and life forms. Much of the art of applying Feng Shui lies in interpreting the natural imagery associated with each section of the Magic Square.

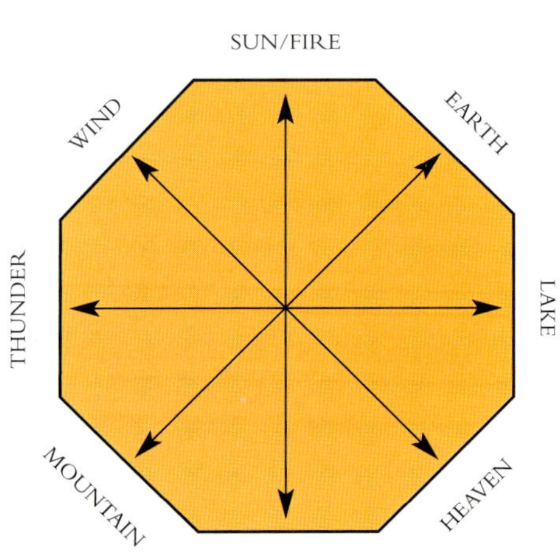

◀ *This arrangement shows how the dynamic forces of the universe interact to create life.*

We can interpret these natural phenomena at their face value or can read into them ancient concepts describing the workings of the universe. For example, scientists investigating the beginnings of life on Earth believe that huge storms were a catalyst which sparked life into action in the waters. This can be read into the interaction of the opposites Thunder and Lake on the diagram. In the same vein, the interaction of Sun and Water brings about photosynthesis in plants which enable the planet to breathe and on which all living things depend. The Wind, the Sun's rays and rain from the skies (Heaven) bring this about, while the Earth and Mountain create a stable and nourishing environment in which life forms can thrive.

▶ *Rice terraces in China follow the contours of the mountains, showing how human beings can work in harmony with Nature.*

In ancient China, garden designers were inspired by the wonderful mountain formations and the water-filled valleys. Poets wrote about mountains, seen from near and far, from above and below, and rocks were placed in gardens so that they could be seen from different vantage points. Scenes were designed to change with the seasons and the weather, and garden buildings and walkways were designed to take in these different views. Rocks and buildings were placed high on hills or mounds where they could be seen from a distance, or low in valleys, by lakes and pools. All the garden features were contained in large open spaces, within which smaller vistas opened up.

▲ *Zigzag walkways are designed to offer different views of the garden as they twist and turn through it.*

◀ *The Moon Gate invites us to move beyond our immediate space, symbolically opening up our vision.*

The Four Animals

The classic Four Animal formation governs the placement of each building and each vista in a garden. The backdrop, in the Tortoise position, is something solid, like a clump of pine trees or a rock, with trees and shrubs or more rocks to the east in the Dragon position. To the west, the area should be lower and flatter to keep the unpredictable energy of the Tiger under control, and in front, in the Phoenix position, should be a small clump of trees or a small rock to mark the boundary of the garden space.

YIN AND YANG

Nowhere is the duality of the two opposing yet complementary forces of yin and yang more pronounced than in the garden. The strong, solid mountains, or the rocks which represent them, contrast with the still, deep waters in the lakes and ponds. The image portrayed by each would not be so effective if they were not set in contrast to each other. The beauty of a single flower is more pronounced when set against a dark, rocky surface, as are the twisted branches of an ancient tree when seen against the sky.

There is a feeling of serenity in a Chinese garden, but not because it is lifeless and still. There is movement and also sound – the rustle of the wind through the trees and the call of birds and animals. Movement is suggested by the shapes of the rocks, which may be given evocative names like Crouching Tiger and Flying Dragon, as well as in the patterns within the weathered rock faces. The bent trunks and twisted stems of carefully positioned

▲ *An example of yin and yang – solidity and emptiness. The path tempts us forward.*

◀ *Solid rocks set off delicate plants and a tiny spray of water that wets the pebbles.*

▼ *The twisted stems of* Corylus avellana *'Contorta' would be lost against foliage but stand out against a white wall.*

Yin Plants	Yang Plants
Apricot	Bamboo (below)
Jasmine	Cherry
Magnolia	Chrysanthemum
Pear	Orchid
Rhododendron	Peony
Rose (below)	Willow

trees and shrubs contrast with pale walls or the sky. Ancient Chinese gardens provided the backdrop for social life in wealthy circles. Operas, dancing and music filled the gardens with sound. They were lit by lanterns which created their own tableaux.

Everything in a Chinese garden is strategically placed to highlight its beauty and impact and is seen in relation to everything else around it. An English cottage garden, filled with a rich variety of flowers, is lovely in a completely different way to one in which a beautiful stone or a single bloom is all that is needed to create a powerful visual impact. Every plant is endowed with yin or yang

▼ *A wooden arch acts as a Moon Gate to beckon us to a different part of the garden.*

▲ *A small rock and a pool can take on the characteristics of a mountain and a lake.*

Yang	Yin
People	Nature
Narrow	Broad
Hard	Soft
Dominant	Supportive
Straight	Curved
Solidity	Emptiness
Movement	Stillness
High	Low
Visible	Concealed
Exterior	Interior

depending on its qualities or the symbolism of the character which represents it in the Chinese language.

Perspective is used in an interesting way in the Chinese garden. Vistas like those created by the great Western landscape designers are an integral part of Chinese design, but there is an additional emphasis. Sizes are seen to be relative. A vast mountain viewed from a distance can appear small, but a small stone close at hand can be given great importance. The notion of the "garden room", which has been part of Western design for a number of years, is also a traditional feature of Chinese gardens. Small gardens are created within larger spaces and larger vistas are opened up within quite small areas by using "windows" to give glimpses of the world beyond.

The Island of the Immortals

Ponds and lakes often contain an island in imitation of the sacred dwelling place of the Eight Immortals far off in the eastern seas. It is designed to lure them into the garden to reveal the secrets of eternal life. Trees are never planted on islands since this would symbolize isolation.

CHI – THE UNIVERSAL ENERGY

Chi is the life force present in all animate beings and is also the subtle energy expressed by seemingly inanimate objects. Gardens reflect the human quest for longevity, which in China means the maintenance of youth, rather than the Western concept of being long-lived. Every feature in a garden is placed there to achieve this aim; rocks and lakes represent permanence, and long-lived trees, shrubs and perennial plants are preferred to annuals or biennials. This makes the chi, the life force of the environment, strong and stable.

Rocks

Rocks are symbolic of the mountains which are the dominant features of many parts of China. Three types of rock were incorporated into the design of large classical gardens – huge rocks big enough to walk through, delicate upright rocks and those which had complex patterns or shapes. Rockeries were built in the north and west of gardens to provide shelter and to act as a contrast to pools, which were situated in the south and east to capture the beneficial energies believed to emanate from those directions.

Rocks may appear to be inanimate, but the Chinese perceive them to be powerful and to speak volumes in the veining on their surfaces and the symbolic expressions suggested by their shapes. Small stones, known as dreamstones, are set into the backs of chairs and hung on walls in garden pavilions. As objects for contemplation, they can lead us, via the energy channels in their markings, to pursue the Tao in our quest to be at one with the universe.

Water

Water brings energy to a garden. A still pond reflects the ever-changing heavens, and brings in the energy of the universe and the sun, the moon, the stars and the clouds that are reflected on the surface. Moving water brings sound and movement as it tumbles over pebbles and creates small whirlpools and eddies. Fountains did not feature in ancient Chinese gardens, but modern technology enables us to bring the energy of water into even the tiniest space.

Water symbolizes wealth and is believed to be a good collector and conductor of chi. Gently flowing water, entering a healthy pool from the east, is very auspicious, particularly when it meanders slowly away and cannot be seen leaving. Gold and silver coloured fish symbolize money and are therefore found in abundance in China. Although pools may be square, the planting should create a kidney-shaped arrangement which appears to hug a building protectively. Symmetrical arrangements do not exist in large Chinese gardens but are acceptable in smaller ones.

▲ *Water is an integral part of a Chinese garden, with a variety of paths and walkways to provide different vistas over it.*

▶ *Bridges with semi-circular arches are common in China. Reflected in the water, the arch creates a circle symbolizing Heaven.*

Paths and Bridges

Paths meander through Chinese gardens, in the open or under covered walkways, gently curving from the east to bring in the auspicious rising energy, or more curved if coming from the west, to slow down the falling, depleted energy associated with that direction. Arched bridges span waterways, creating perfect circles with their reflections in the water, symbolizing Heaven. Others zigzag, an odd number of twists being yang and offering a soft yin vista of still water and plants. An even number of twists is yin, offering a yang view of rocks or buildings. Pagodas are often placed in the north-east and the south-west, sometimes referred to as "Doors of the Devil", to keep evil influences at bay, as these are the directions of the prevailing winds.

Trees and Plants

The planting in Chinese gardens is permanent so that the trees and plants build up an energetic relationship with their environment. We may find it strange that colour is not given special consideration, except when it reflects the passing of the seasons, but it is incidental to the main purpose of the Chinese garden.

▼ *The walkway at Jiangling Museum, China, links the building to its surroundings and offers different vistas as it zigzags.*

▼ *An unobscured outside window such as this links the inner world of the house with the outer world beyond.*

▼ *The same window seen from the inside shows how the link is maintained and the garden beckons us outside.*

Buildings and Structures

Since people are an integral part of the garden, pavilions and decks are important features, encouraging them to congregate and pursue leisure interests. Bridges, paths and covered walkways give access to vistas and secluded places and enable people to enjoy gentle exercise. Walls and doorways link the inner world of the house with the outer world beyond.

Furniture and Other Objects

Seats and pots feature in the Chinese garden, but the main focus is on the rocks and the plants. In public gardens, amusing objects like huge colourful dragons appear at festival times. In parks, vivid beds of brightly coloured plants, often with swirling designs incorporated, reflect the public, or yang, space as opposed to the yin space of the private garden.

THE FIVE ELEMENTS

The Five Elements of Wood, Fire, Earth, Metal and Water are the agents of chi and they represent shapes, colours, and the senses. The aim in the Feng Shui garden is to create a space where no one element is dominant and in which there is a balance of yin and yang. The feel of a garden is very different when a balance exists, and we can achieve this in our planting schemes and by careful placement of garden buildings and ornaments. This is not to say that a garden must have something of every colour, or of every shape. There is an old Chinese saying, "Too many colours blind the eye", and we have all seen gardens that are full of brightly coloured plants, ornaments and features. They make an incredible visual show and grab the attention of passers-by, but are not conducive to relaxation or harmony.

The Feng Shui garden follows the example of the natural world in striving for a balance between shape and colour. It gives us the scope to experiment and introduce our favourite exotic plants or outlandish sculptures as well as intriguing garden buildings or brightly coloured walls – provided the perspective, proportions and balance are right. See "The Relationships of the Five Elements" table for details of the balancing elements.

▼ Any plant, regardless of its shape or size, represents the Wood element. Tall, upright trees symbolize the Wood element shape.

▲ These three examples of Fire shapes – the cordyline, the potted conifers and the clipped bay – each have a different energy.

Wood

All plants represent the Wood element which obviously dominates the planting in any garden, yet the shapes and colours of the plants and the settings in which we place them can suggest other elements. To introduce the Wood element specifically, we can use columnar trees and trellis with upright wooden supports.

Fire

Fire is suggested in plants with pointed leaves and the introduction of even a single specimen can transform a lifeless bed.

▼ The rounded domes on this hedge suggest Metal but the meandering shape is Water, which follows Metal in the elemental cycle.

Five Element Features in the Garden

	Wood	Fire	Earth	Metal	Water
Colour	Green	Red Purple	Yellow Orange Brown	White Silver	Dark blue Black
Represen-tations	Columns Furniture Decking Planters Logs	Pyramids Obelisks Arrows Points Lights	Rectangles Flat tops Squares Troughs Rock and stone	Domes Balls Hummocks Bowls Lead	Meanders Drifts Gravel Water features Glass

Triangles and pyramid shapes are also representative of Fire and many supports for climbing plants are available in this shape. When siting them, be careful that they are not out of proportion to the structures and plants surrounding them. The Fire element is powerful. A splash of red which represents this element is enough to make a definite statement.

Earth

Earth is suggested in paving and pathway materials. The real thing – the garden soil – is not on show in the Feng Shui garden since it will be covered with plants. Flat-topped fences, trellises and walkways suggest the Earth element. Too much of this shape can depress the chi of a place and it can easily dominate a garden surrounded by walls and fences. Introduce different shapes in garden buildings and structures and attempt to alter the shape of the view.

▼ *The metal shapes of these trees appear to dance, bringing a lively energy to the garden.*

Metal

Round shapes and domes represent the Metal element. The yin and yang aspects of this in the garden can be very different. Tall, closely packed oval conifers can be menacing to walk through. On the other hand, a series of small coniferous balls spread around the garden introduce an element of fun. All-white gardens can have a lifeless feel about them but in a small conservatory they have a pleasantly cooling effect.

Water

Apart from the real thing, the Water element is suggested by meandering shapes, both in paths and in planting. Gravel and heather gardens are an example of Water-shaped planting and similar effects can be achieved by low planting or by introducing drifts of the same plant or colours.

▲ *Low, meandering planting suggests the Water element, as it resembles a stream.*

The Transformation of the Elements

Just as yin and yang each transform into the other when their energy reaches its peak, so can the Elements transform into their opposites. The best example of this in the garden is where the Wood element transforms into Earth. In a predominantly green garden, with Earth-shaped boundaries and brown, wooden, rectangular furniture, the Wood is transformed into the Earth element and the result is a low-energy garden. The remedy is to introduce other shapes and splashes of colour to bring the garden to life.

THE UNSEEN ENERGIES

There are many unseen energies at work in the garden. Some manifest themselves in physical conditions which we can observe. Others, if we are unaware of them, can create difficulties when we are sitting and working in the garden. Many, however, work for our benefit and we must take care to create a safe haven for them.

UNDERGROUND WATER

There may be some areas in the garden which are situated over underground water sources. We need to be aware of this in order to choose plants which will survive in such conditions – it is no use putting in plants which prefer dry conditions here. Such areas will have a bearing on how we design the garden and we should mark them on any plan we make.

Underground streams can create a disturbance in the earth which may affect plants growing above them and could have an adverse effect on us if we are sitting or working above them for any length of time. Dowsing is the best way to find these and it may be worth engaging a dowser to check an area before you build a garden office or workshop. Distressed plants – trees which lean for no apparent reason, shrubs which develop cankers or plants which look sickly and die for no obvious reason – reveal that something is amiss.

▲ *Underground water can create difficulties in gardens in terms of geopathic stress and waterlogged areas.*

► *Trees have a relationship with their environment and provide a home to thousands of different species of animals and plants.*

▼ *If you respect the garden's natural ecological system you will be rewarded with a garden full of healthy, beautiful plants.*

THE SOIL

Our greatest ally in the garden is healthy soil. Before we plant anything we need to ensure that the soil is right for the plants we want to grow. Nurseries sell soil-testing kits and gardening books provide advice on the suitability of plants for

▶ *Ancient peoples ran their lives by the movement of the stars and watched the skies for signs to plant and harvest crops.*

specific conditions. Acid-loving plants will never thrive in alkaline soil and vice versa. A Feng Shui garden should go with the flow. It is virtually impossible to alter the soil permanently in order to grow your favourite plants, so before buying a new house it is worth looking in neighbouring gardens to see which plants do well in the area.

The soil is a living entity teeming with millions of micro-organisms, each with its own role to play in the ecology of the garden. In the Feng Shui garden these microbes are valued and we should provide them with the conditions in which to thrive, in terms of sun, rain and air, as well as food made from composting our garden and kitchen waste. The folly of planting through plastic or microporous sheeting, which prevents weeds but also suffocates the micro-organisms and causes the soil to become stagnant and lifeless, is now understood.

Spirit of the Place

Some people believe that trees and plants are imbued with spirits. Others respect the relationship that long-lived trees have built up with the Earth and the support and nourishment that they provide for micro-organisms, other plants and animals, including human beings. Every garden has its support team of mammals, birds and insects, and even snails, which have a role. The slightest tinkering in terms of chemicals or soil disturbance can have an unsettling effect on the ecological chain. In the Feng Shui garden we respect our fellow workers.

Cosmic Energies

Ancient peoples around the world respected the part played by the sun, the moon and the weather in their lives and the growth of their crops, and many festivals reflect this. The cosmos affects who we are and determines our characters. This also applies in the plant world although plants cannot take charge and manipulate circumstances as we can. We must determine the best conditions for them. By planting according to the movements of the moon, we can greatly improve the conditions for our plants. Planting by the moon's phases is an ancient skill and requires only watching the sky or consulting a diary giving the dates of the new and full moons.

▼ *The new moon – time to plant annual flower seeds, leafy vegetables and cereals.*

▶ *The numbered days correspond to the days of the moon's cycle. It is advisable not to plant close to the equinoxes and the solstices.*

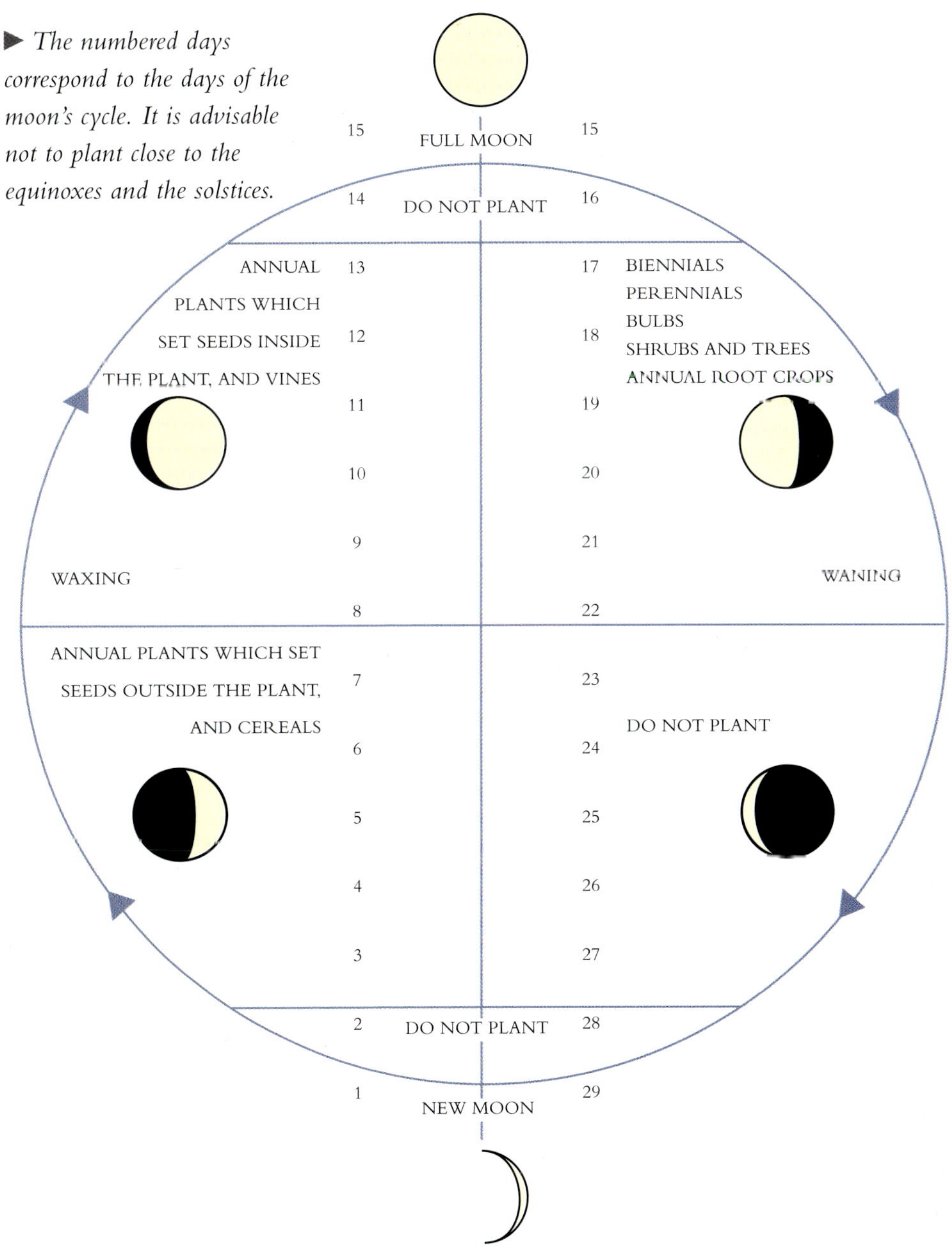

THE SHAPE OF THE GARDEN

▲ *This picket fence defines the space and acts as a boundary without shutting out the world to a garden full of energy. The whole effect would be improved by taking out the dead tree on the right.*

The shape of the plot of land on which we build, or on which our existing home is sited, is important in Feng Shui. Regular shapes are best, so that there are no missing areas. We can use various means to make a plot appear more regular in shape than it already is. Fences and trellis can divide awkwardly-shaped plots into separate areas which are easier to deal with individually. The use of different materials as edging can create boundaries and, of course, plants can open up or conceal the most difficult spaces. Creative planting can create virtually any illusion we desire.

▼ *Trellis can be used to divide up gardens which have difficult shapes.*

▼ *This house sits well in its plot. The back gardens of houses built in Britain over the past century tend to be larger than the front but in most of Europe and in the United States, the reverse is true. Trees and shrubs protect the rear and sides and a fence shields the front, in line with the classic Four Animals formation.*

▼ *This house sits too far to the back of its plot. The tall trees here will be overwhelming to the occupants of the house and from a more practical point of view could even be dangerous in high winds. Local preservation orders should be checked before taking steps to reduce the height of the trees.*

▲ *By changing the shape of the plot within the garden and with careful planting, the harsh lines of a triangular plot are lessened.*

▲ *Trellis or other features, preferably rounded, will serve to reduce the effect of the triangle's points. Mirrors in the positions indicated (A and B) reflect interesting planting, not each other, and will give the illusion of pushing the boundaries out.*

The Rectangular Plot

A rectangular plot is regarded as the ideal shape. The house should be sited on the centre of the plot so that the garden is in proportion around the house.

The Triangular Plot

Triangular plots are not considered desirable in Feng Shui because the sharp points are felt to resemble knives. They are also difficult to deal with because they create three areas of stagnant energy. However, with careful planting and the erection of screens, it is possible to create the illusion of a regular shaped plot. An alternative is to plant heavily on the boundaries and use meandering paths within the garden.

Round and L-shaped Plots

Round plots are difficult. Although the chi is able to flow freely round, it is difficult to contain it and it is advisable to create other, more stable shapes within the circle for seating areas. L-shaped and other irregularly shaped plots are best divided into regular shaped sections to make them simpler to deal with.

The Bright Hall

The Bright Hall was originally a pool of water in front of a house. Its function was to gather energy and to preserve an open space there. It could take the form of a sunken garden or simply an open, gathering space. These days it is the space in front of the front door. It should be in proportion to the front of the house, and be well maintained and uncluttered.

▲ *The chi flows quickly around this circular plot. Contain it with a shrub hedge and create inner areas for seating.*

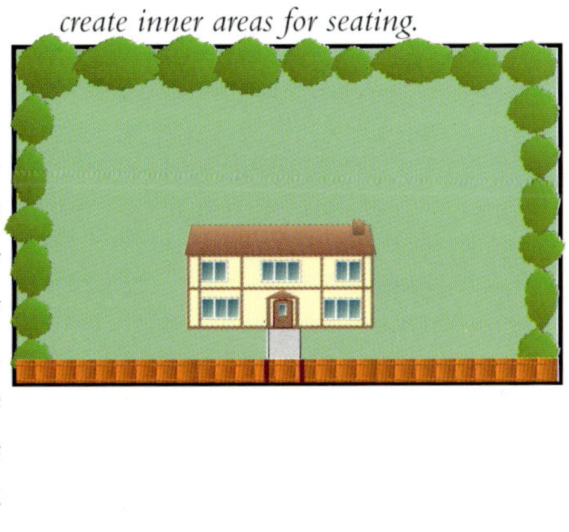

▲ *A trellis or fence positioned as shown will regularize this L-shaped plot.*

CASE STUDY

Care has to be taken when designing a Bright Hall, as Tom and Rhoda discovered. They created a wonderful Bright Hall in front of their house. Made of mellow stone and edged with red brick, which blended with the house, it was welcoming and greatly enhanced the front entrance. However, a Chinese Feng Shui consultant pronounced it inauspicious and suggested they have a straight step instead. They were flabbergasted but the reason was that on coming out of the house, the round edge turned into the lip of a jug, symbolically pouring money away down the sloping drive and into the road.

Some people have a greater level of perception than others but the skill can be acquired with practice. Before building or planting we should mark out our ideas and view them from all angles.

▲ *Viewed from the front this well-built Bright Hall appears to create a welcoming space in front of the house.*

▲ *However, seen from this angle, it resembles the lip of a jug, symbolically pouring money away.*

DRAWING THE PLAN

Before creating a Feng Shui garden it is first necessary to investigate the compass directions around the site to determine the direction of the prevailing winds and to site the plants according to their preferences. When we are sitting or working in the garden it is useful to place ourselves in auspicious directions. We also need to investigate the positions of the Five Elements of the site to create a balance between them and with the features which we place in the garden.

Draw a Plan

Using graph paper to a suitable scale, take measurements for the length and breadth of the garden and mark

- ◆ House and garage
- ◆ Walls and fences
- ◆ Large trees and shrubs
- ◆ Garden buildings
- ◆ Semi-permanent features such as ponds, rockeries and patios.
- ◆ Features in the surrounding environment such as trees, other buildings, lampposts and so on.

Take a Compass Reading

1. Remove watches, jewellery and metal objects and stand clear of cars and other metal fixtures.

2. Stand with your back parallel to the front door and note the exact compass reading in degrees.

3. Note the direction, e.g. 349° North, and mark it on to the plan of the garden as shown in the diagram. You are now ready to transfer the compass readings on to your Bagua drawing.

4. Place the protractor on the Bagua diagram so that 0° is at the bottom at the North position.

5. Find the compass reading for your home and check you have the corresponding direction – if not you may be reading the wrong ring.

6. Mark the position of your house.

7. Look at the "Directions" table on the opposite page to double check the compass direction.

Transfer the Directions to the Plan

1. To find the centre of the plan, match the main boundaries across the length of the plan and crease the paper lengthways.

2. Match the main boundaries across the width and crease the paper widthways.

3. Where the folds of the creases cross

You Will Need

- ◆ A scale plan of your home. If you own your home you will already have one. If not, it will be necessary to draw one, in which case you will also need a tape measure and graph paper
- ◆ A compass with the eight directions clearly marked
- ◆ A ruler
- ◆ A lead pencil and five coloured pencils – green, red, yellow, grey, dark blue
- ◆ A tracing of the Bagua with the suggested information marked on
- ◆ A protractor

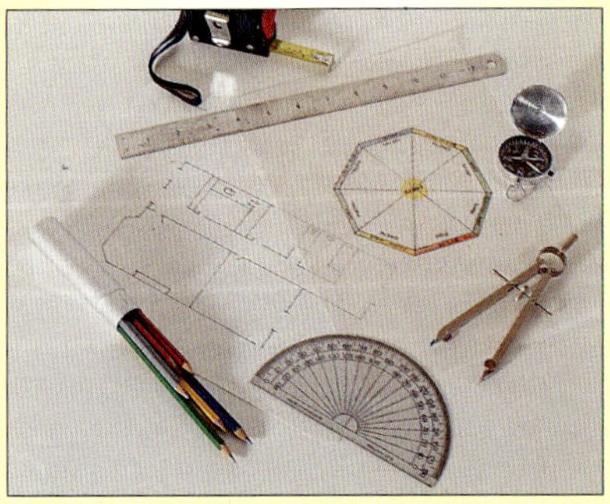

▼ *The Bagua should be superimposed on the plan to line up the main entrance with its corresponding direction and element.*

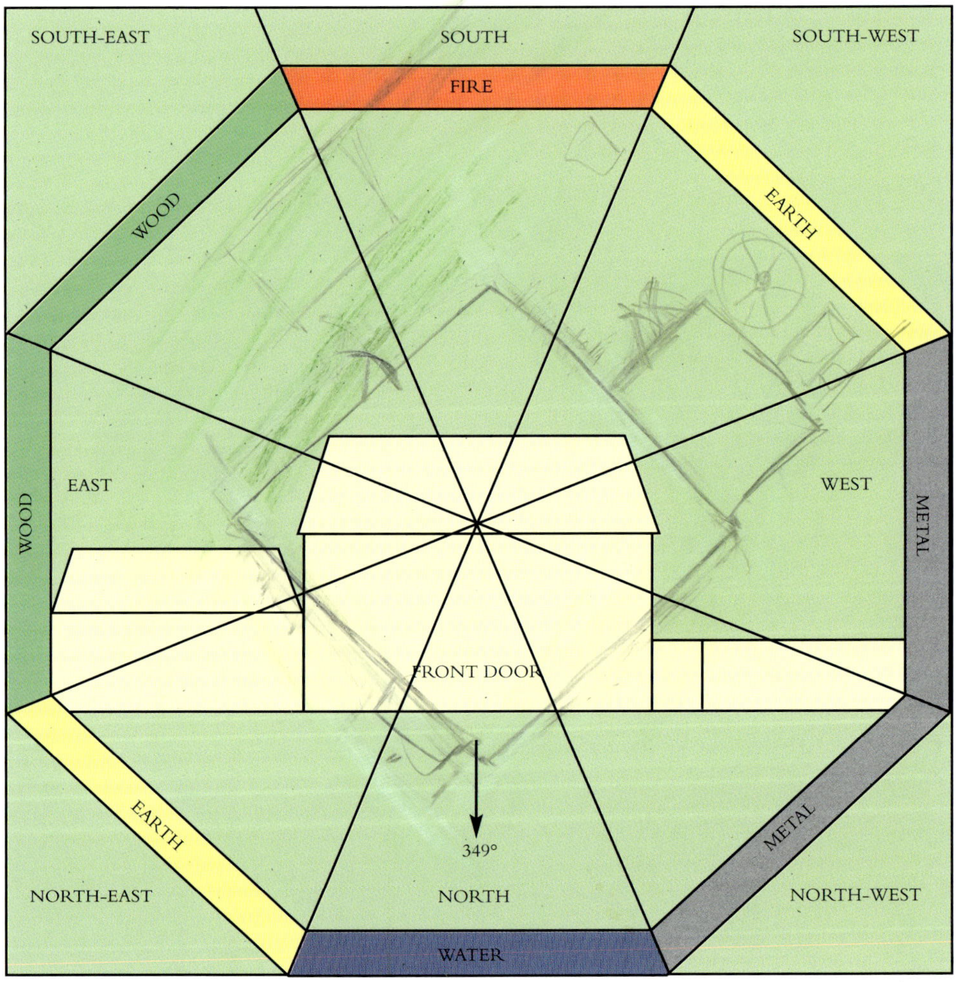

Directions	
North	337.5 – 22.5°
North-east	22.5 – 67.5°
East	67.5 – 112.5°
South-east	112.5 – 157.5°
South	157.5 – 202.5°
South-west	202.5 – 247.5°
West	247.5 – 292.5°
North-west	292.5 – 337.5°

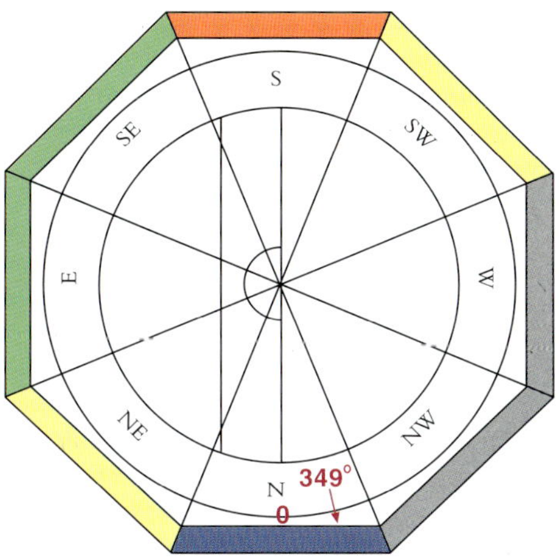

▲ *A circular protractor will help you line up the compass direction and the Bagua.*

► *Semi permanent features like this pond, and all buildings and boundaries, should be marked on the plan.*

marks the centre of your garden.

4. If your garden is not a perfect square or rectangular shape, treat a protrusion less than 50% of the width as an extension to the direction.

5. If the protrusion is more than 50% of the width, treat the remainder as a missing part of the direction.

6. Place the centre of the Bagua on the centre point of the plan and line up the front door position.

7. Mark the eight directions on the plan and draw in the sectors.

8. Transfer the Bagua's colour markings on to the plan.

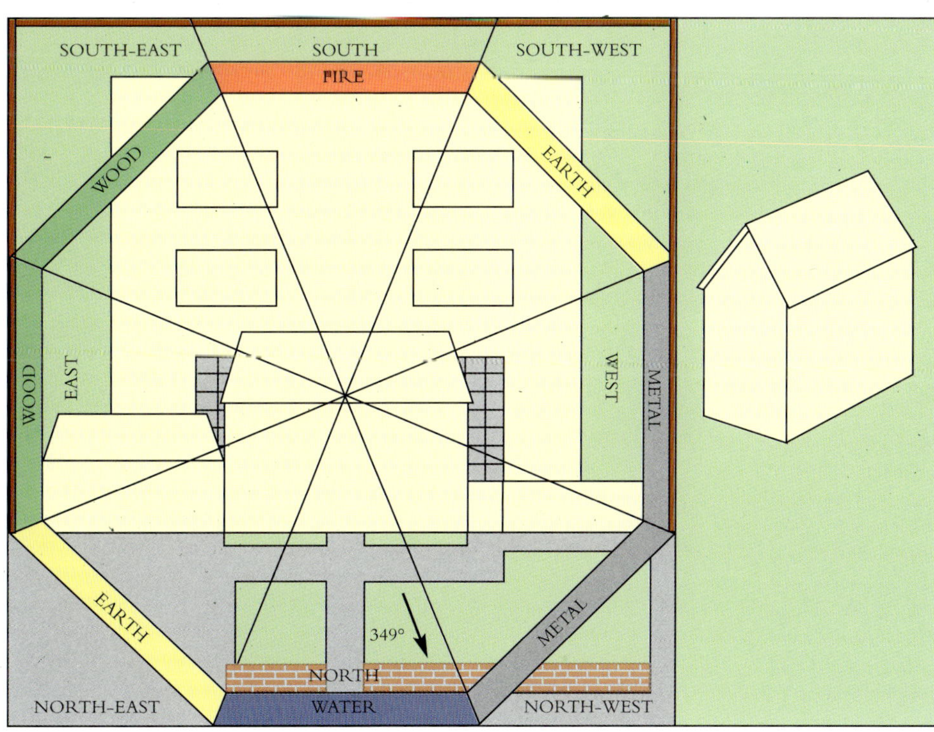

► *Once you have marked on the exisitng main features of your plot you will be ready to investigate the Feng Shui potential of your garden.*

CASE STUDY

Mike and Sarah wanted a more interesting garden which required as little maintenance as possible. The neighbours on their left complained that the four-year-old *Cupressocyparis leylandii* trees were blocking their light and those on the right that they were killing near-by plants. Mike came to realize that they were a high-maintenance feature as they grew so fast. With three sons under the age of 12, they required a large space for ball games. Sarah wanted to grow some fruit and a few summer salad vegetables.

▼ *Once you know your magic number you can determine which directions are beneficial and will support you. Whether you are relaxing in the garden or enjoying a meal with family or friends you can choose to place your chair to face your best direction.*

Where to Sit	
1	SE or N
2	NE or SW
3	S or E
4	N or SE
5(m)	NE or SW
5(f)	SW or NE
6	W or NW
7	NW or W
8	E or S
9	E or S

▲ *While not exactly looking after themselves, interesting gardens like this require reasonably low maintenance.*

▼ *Water features come in many shapes and sizes and, placed in auspicious positions, can bring good luck and focus thought.*

▼ *We can bring water into the garden even in the smallest space, as illustrated by this Japanese-style water feature.*

The family wanted a low-maintenance pond to attract wildlife. Sarah also wanted a water feature on the patio.

Much to everyone's relief, the *leylandii* were removed and the soil was improved with organic matter and compost.

1. The four "cornerstones" were addressed first. In the south-west, an ivy-covered trellis was erected to filter the wind. A solid hedge would have set up wind turbulence.

2. A blossom tree was placed on the lawn to filter the north-east wind and to encourage the vibrant energy of the east on to the site.

3. A closed-back arbour was placed in the south-east to hide the compost bins, ideally placed in the Wealth area to provide sustenance for the garden, and to stabilize the area. The Fire-shaped roof moves the energy forward.

4. In the north-west a rounded metal plate was positioned showing the number of the house.

5. A light is placed in the north-east.

6. A rockery is sited in the Phoenix position in the front garden.

7. The path meanders to a spacious step, and pots with round-shaped plants as guardians sit on either side of the door.

8. A shrub is grown on the wall between the garage and house to help reduce the impact of a north-east wind.

9. A shrub here balances the one on the other side.

10. A yellow-berried pyracantha is placed here to stimulate the Metal energy and to give some prickly protection against unwelcome intruders.

11. A meandering stepping-stone path leads from the garage and the side gate, giving a balanced formality to the garden but affording different vistas as it curves.

12. The large back lawn area is surrounded by trees and shrubs – staggered, like fielders, to catch the children's stray balls and also to provide a pleasant walk around the garden.

13. The pond is backed by evergreen plants and shrubs to prevent leaves from falling into it. Situated in the south-west it signifies future prosperity and should be kept healthy with oxygenating plants.

14. On a square wooden table stands a round metal sundial with an arrow pointing upwards. Every one of the Five Elements is used here to stimulate the Fame and Future Possibilities area of the symbolic Bagua.

15. Sarah places perennial plants and bulbs in an urn in front of the arbour – silver and gold to represent money in the summer months and red berries in the winter months to stimulate the Wealth area of the Symbolic Bagua.

16. A medium-height evergreen tree is planted here which will eventually block the point of the roof of a neighbouring house. Meanwhile, a concave mirror is placed on the side of the house to symbolically absorb the "poison arrow".

17. Trellis is erected around the edge of a paved area to protect the house from any thrown balls and to enable Sarah to grow espalier-trained fruit. Herbs are grown in the flower beds as companion plants and salad vegetables are grown in the gaps.

18. A small water feature in the east stimulates the area of current prosperity.

19. Sarah's small greenhouse enables her to overwinter her perennial pot plants.

20. The patio chairs are positioned so that Sarah and Mike are backed by the garage wall, facing favourable positions. The protective Four Animal arrangement corresponds to the back, front and side aspects of the house and not to actual compass directions.

USING THE BAGUA IN THE GARDEN

▲ *A garden full of energy – different shapes, colours and levels, and a variety of materials, add to the interest.*

The symbolic Bagua is generally discussed in terms of the house, yet we can use its magic in the garden too. If there is a certain aspect of our lives on which we need to focus, the symbolic Bagua gives us a tool to stimulate the energy associated with it, particularly when we look out on the area through the kitchen or sitting room windows. As in the house, we can divide the garden into rooms when applying the Bagua since it is not usual to be able to see the whole garden from one vantage point.

The enhancements used are designed to focus the mind and to create a stabilizing effect by using or alluding to heavy objects such as stones or mountains, or to shift something in our lives by creating or alluding to movement, water, or wind-blown items. Empty pots and

▲ *A herb garden directly outside a window is a good area to apply the Bagua.*

◀ *Use pots of plants in a group as a focus point in the garden.*

SUGGESTIONS FOR ENHANCEMENTS:

- ◆ Rocks, stones and large pots for added stability
- ◆ Wind objects to stir up the energy and create movement
- ◆ Fountains and water features for abundance
- ◆ Empty urns and dishes to accept the gifts of the universe
- ◆ Lights to illuminate paths or particular features in the garden
- ◆ Collections and art works for achievement
- ◆ Pot plants for focus

CASE STUDY

Paul and Claire both work from home. Paul is a writer who has had two novels published. He would like a more settled life, with a regular contract with a publisher, and would like to branch out and write for TV. Claire runs an aromatherapy practice and is planning to develop an idea and sell products by mail order. They both adore gardening and, when they are not in their respective study or workrooms, they spend much of their leisure time there. They have enhanced the appropriate areas of the Bagua in their home and would like to do the same in the garden.

1. Paul placed a bird table in the Helpful People area of the small side garden outside his office window in order to encourage the calls from publishers and TV companies to roll in. As organic gardeners, Paul and Claire do not like spraying insect pests, so small birds are very welcome in the garden. Paul greased the pole of the table to keep the birds safe from cats and prevent squirrels from taking the food. He takes care to observe which plants the birds are attracted to naturally and uses seeds from those plants to feed them, since he feels that bread and commercially produced bird food may harm them. He also places a dish of clean water there every day.

2. In the Fame area, Paul placed a large terracotta sun which smiles at him when he looks up from his work and will hopefully help him to fulfil his ambitions.

3. In the small garden outside Claire's therapy room, she placed a dish containing her rock plant collection in the Offspring area in order to focus on her business plans.

4. On the trellis separating Claire's garden from the main garden, the couple planted a *Trachelospermum jasminoides* – an evergreen climbing plant with fragrant white flowers which will last for most of the summer. This is in the Offspring area of the main garden.

5. Opposite the climber, Paul and Claire created a pond with a fountain, in the Family area of the main garden, having first checked that the water was not in an inauspicious position with regard to the Five Elements.

urns can suggest an empty space waiting for something to happen – this is particularly helpful in the Wealth area, for example. Whatever image we use must have meaning for us in that we can see it physically and relate to its illusion and symbolism. Thus we should use images from our own culture and experience. Whatever we use should not clash with the element of the direction, but if possible should strengthen it. A pot of plants suggesting the colour of the element can always be used, or an enhancement suggested on the facing page.

Since the enhancements are meant to trigger an emotion or action, we should place them where we can see them. If we have a large front garden, gardens to the side and at the back of the house, the chances are that there will be areas which we rarely look at. Those areas which are more useful to us in placing the Bagua are those which we constantly look at. For example, if we have a herb garden outside the kitchen window, or if our study faces the side garden, then these are the areas to concentrate on.

GARDEN FEATURES

For the most part we cannot determine the natural phenomena in our gardens or in the wider environment. We are, however, responsible for the plants and features we install there. With an understanding of the principles which govern Feng Shui, we can choose furniture, buildings, plants and colours which work in harmony with each other and the surrounding area and which create a balanced and supportive environment for us. We can also deliberately introduce features which clash in order to create a more vibrant energy in the garden.

PATHS

Paths carry chi through the garden and their size, shape and the materials they are made of can affect the movement of the energy. This will affect the way we feel about and perceive the space.

Front Gardens

Generally speaking, paths lead to entrances, doors or gates. When they are straight, they channel energy quickly so we tend not to notice the garden and instead simply move between our homes and the outside world. In the Feng Shui garden, the aim is to use the front garden

▼ *There are points of interest all along this gently curving path.*

▲ *Winding paths slow us down and allow us to observe the garden. Note how the spiky potted plants bring this garden to life.*

as a space between home and the outside world where we can gather energy in the morning and slow down at the end of a hard day.

To enable us to slow down, paths should gently curve or meander, presenting us with different angles and views as we move along them. If we have no control over the shape of the path, then placing pots along them or planting so that the lines of a straight path are broken up by overhanging plants are possible alternatives. Another option is to make breaks every so often, either with beds containing plants or some kind of ornamental feature, or by creating a visual barrier using different materials.

Back Gardens

Paths should also meander around the back garden so that we constantly happen upon different views. Ideally, we

▲ *This straight path channels chi to and from the door far too quickly.*

▲ *This curving path slows down the chi and offers us different views.*

▲ *Pots spaced along a straight path will help to slow down the chi.*

▲ *Straight paths broken up in this way help to slow the energy down.*

▲ *The use of different materials also helps to slow down the energy.*

should not be able to take in the whole area in one glance. Where gardens are large, paths can tantalizingly draw us through gaps in trees, walls and trellises into other garden rooms beyond. Offices and sheds are places to which we often need to get in a hurry. A straight path is acceptable here, but in the case of the home office, an alternative, meandering route would be ideal.

▲ *This meandering path gives the right impression but is a little too narrow.*

Materials for Paths

Stone blocks (below), Brick, Gravel, Cobbles, Tiles, Bark, Wood, Concrete slabs, Grass

Materials

Paths need to be stable and suited to their purpose. In a large garden they may need to carry heavy barrows, and therefore deep gravel would not be suitable. Cobble stones are not suitable path materials in the homes of elderly or disabled people since stability is especially important. Materials can vary in suitability between different areas – for instance in a wooded area bark paths with log edgings are fine, but grass paths and smooth surfaces are not a good idea in such damp places as they become slippery.

The materials we use will depend on local architectural style and we should aim to harmonize with it. Coloured concrete might blend into a modern urban garden but would look out of place in a rural garden, as would mellow weathered stone in an urban basement. Although the materials chosen must blend with the surroundings, we can make our paths individual by blending different materials into the design. Brick edging for concrete paths or the use of two different coloured bricks are just two of many ideas we can use.

Crazy paving is rarely used in the Feng Shui garden since its broken appearance symbolizes instability. However, it does feature in ancient Chinese gardens. Where crazy paving is well-laid, on a stable concrete foundation, the joints do not crack and the paving does not lift, it can be safely used.

▲ *Although straight, this wide pathway is practical in the herb and vegetable garden – and the plants hang over to slow down the flow of energy.*

▼ *Hidden pathways in different materials – which one should we take?*

BOUNDARIES

We all need boundaries in order to feel protected and safe. As children, our boundaries are formed by the family unit and, as we get older, they expand to include school, our work and the organizations we join. When we become adults we continue to live within the boundaries of our social, recreational and professional groups. Our most important space is our home where we go to be ourselves and for support and rest. Boundaries are important in our relationships with our neighbours and with the world at large, as demarcation lines which give us a sense of security.

▲ *A front garden divides the home from the outside world but maintains a connection.*

Front Gardens

In China, the ideal is to have an open view in front of a building, with a small barrier to mark the boundary and, of course, to be facing south. In the West, the reverse is often the case and in temperate climates most people prefer a south-facing back garden. In Feng Shui it is recommended that a front barrier should never exceed the height of the downstairs windowsill, or waist height. To maintain a balance in life, it is important to be able to connect, not only with the immediate outside world but also with the universe, and we should all have a view of the sky and the changing seasons. People who shut themselves off from the world will be at best disenchanted or, at worst, suffer from a depressive illness. Privacy is important but we should not become disconnected from the world or the people in it.

▼ *Boundaries protect us and our homes, but should not cut us off from the world outside.*

Back Gardens

The boundaries we choose for our garden perimeters can act as a backdrop for our plants as well as providing protection. In order for us to feel secure they should be well maintained. Good maintenance helps our relationships with our neighbours, as quarrels over boundaries frequently feature in neighbourly disputes. Thoughtless planting of unsuitable hedging plants, like the fast-growing *Cupressocyparis leylandii*, has been known to result in neighbours ending up in court. Whether we build walls, erect fences or use trees and hedges as our boundaries we need to keep a sense of proportion and plant things which will not outgrow their space or interfere with buildings, other plants or the well-being of our neighbours. If there are insecure areas in the garden perimeter we need to create barriers which will repel intruders. Plants such as holly and pyracantha serve this purpose admirably, but do not place prickly plants where you might brush up against them accidentally.

Smaller boundaries within the garden divide it up into different areas. These can take the form of hedges, fences or trellis, or even a change from grass to flower bed or from path to lawn. We can use a single shrub or a pot to create the illusion of a barrier. Like the Moon Gates in ancient Chinese gardens, gaps in

▼ *A gate such as this gives protection without isolating the home from outside.*

▲ Cupressocyparis leylandii *is a good hedge but needs to be kept under control.*

► *A pyracantha hedge makes an effective, if prickly, barrier.*

hedges, doors in walls and paths through trellis and arbours allow us a glimpse of an area beyond our immediate space. In small gardens the same effect can be achieved by using mirrors and *trompe-l'oeil* designs on walls to draw the eye.

Materials

Boundaries can be created from a variety of materials, or grown, using suitable plants. In either case, skill is required to

Materials for Boundaries

Brick, Pre-cast blocks, Close board wooden panels, Woven wooden panels, Chain link, Post and rail, Wattle hurdles, Split bamboo, Trellis, Chestnut

Hedging Plants for the Side Garden

(1.5–3m/5–10ft)

Cotoneaster simonsii, Berberis stenophylla, Escallonia macrantha, Aucuba japonica

Boundaries and the Five Elements

Fencing materials and shapes can introduce the elements in to your garden. Make sure you balance them with care.

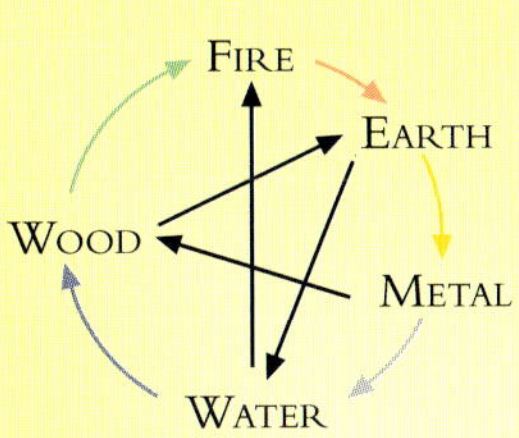

▲ *This is the Destructive Cycle.*

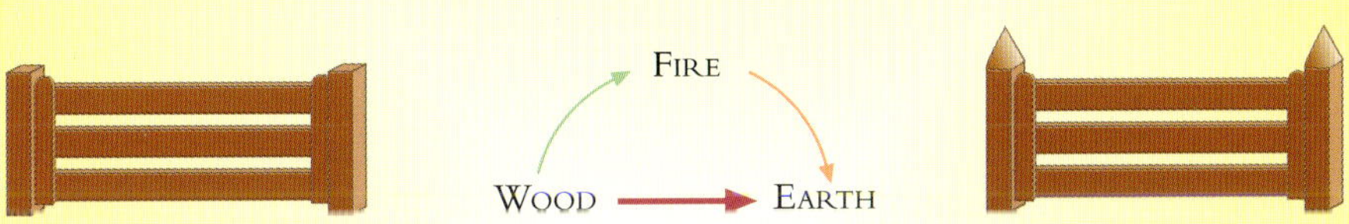

▲ *The first illustration shows the harmful cycle of Wood and Earth. In the second, Fire has been added for balance.*

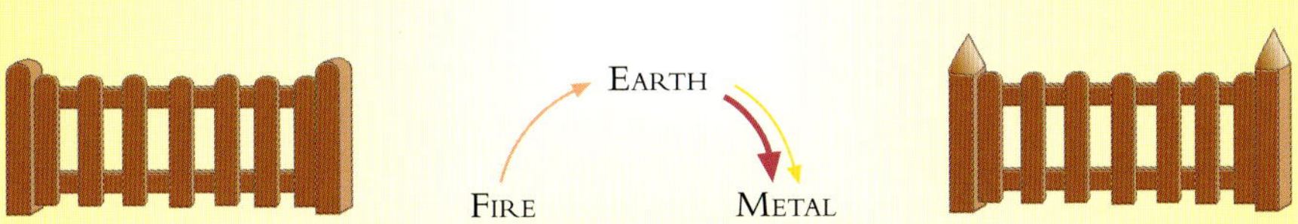

▲ *The first illustration shows the weakening cycle of the elements. In the second Fire has been added as a balance.*

▲ *All the elements are suggested here, but the result is over-elaborate.*

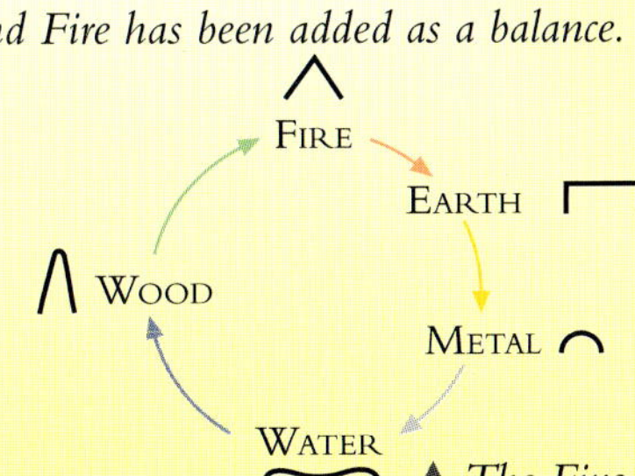

▲ *The Five Element cycle.*

create a visually pleasing and lasting effect. If a plot curves, then placing a straight wall along the boundary will spoil the look. If a hedge is built using mixed planting, incorrect weaving and supports will create a problem for the future. When positioning fences and hedges it is important to remember that windy conditions can affect plants as well as people sitting on the other side of a solid structure. In such places a permeable structure is often preferable. Fencing materials and the finials used on the posts can suggest the shapes of the Five Elements and this needs to be taken into consideration when balancing the elements.

▼ *Old brick walls are a perfect garden backdrop. Complementing materials should be chosen with care, as in this garden.*

WATER IN THE GARDEN

Water is of great importance in Feng Shui. In China it symbolizes the accumulation of chi, which is synonymous with wealth.

Garden Ponds

Any water feature situated near the home should be in proportion to the size of the house. Bigger is not better in this case, since large expanses of water will symbolically drown us. A pond which is too large will dampen our career prospects, and if a fountain is out of proportion we will find it exhausting. Everything in the garden should blend in with existing features and with the landscape. The materials we use are as important as the siting of the feature. Sharp angles could direct "poison arrows" at the house or outdoor seating area.

Whether we live in towns or in the country, our ponds will attract wildlife. Small animals that jump or fall into a pond may not be able to get out again, unless we provide them with some means to do so. If a pond has steep sides, we should make sure that there are rocks or ledges to allow creatures an escape route.

▼ *If you have a stream through the garden slow it down with overhanging plants.*

If there are small children in the household it is important to ensure that ponds are completely safe. It may be better to install another type of water feature until children are old enough to take care.

The ideal shape for ponds is irregular, imitating natural ones. The more irregular the shape, the more plants and wildlife will thrive in and around it.

▲ *Ponds should fit naturally into a garden; irregular shapes with planting work best.*

Round ponds tend to carry the chi away too quickly and square ponds create "poison arrows". Regular shapes are easier to construct, however, and can be softened and shaped into a more natural form by careful planting round the edges.

Rockeries

To balance the yin of a still pond we can introduce the yang energy of a rockery. This combination reflects the mountain and lake formations so important in Chinese philosophy and art and can represent the Tortoise, Dragon and Tiger formation, with the pond in front. The rules for rockery building are:

◆ Use an odd number of stones

◆ Bury the stones by at least a third in the soil

◆ Place stones the correct way up as indicated by the graining

◆ Use a flat stone next to an upright one on its concave side

◆ Line the other stone up with the "toe" of the first

◆ Do not place a round stone by a jagged stone

◆ Choose the most weathered, front "face" of the rock to face forwards

◆ Use the yin and yang theory to create a complementary arrangement

▼ *Rockeries should mirror the natural world and reflect the shape of mountains.*

Water Placement

Ancient Chinese writings set great store by the patterns on the surface of the water, probably as a way of determining the direction of the wind. The Water Dragon Classic, an ancient text, gives details of beneficial places to build amid various shapes of water courses. The direction of the flow determines the best places to plant certain types of crops.

The direction from which water enters or leaves a property is deemed to be crucial, but theories vary. One theory suggests that it should correspond to our auspicious directions. Another suggests that in houses facing north, south, east or west, the water should enter from the east or from left to right in front of the property. Conversely, if a house faces north-east, south-east, north-west or south-west, the water should enter from the west. Another theory favours east since this is the direction of growth.

▲ *The straight sides of this formal garden pond are softened with overhanging plants.*

▲ *A water feature in the south-west of the garden can symbolize future prosperity.*

► *Water trickling towards the house symbolizes wealth rolling in.*

Since few of us have a river running in front of our homes or are in a position to do anything about the flow, we should look at more relevant reasons for siting water features in our gardens.

The major, common-sense rule for water placement is that it should not flow quickly towards you from a point higher than your house because of the danger of flooding. A house built on a flood plain or below sea level might well experience problems, particularly as the effects of global warming cause water levels to continue to rise. It is deemed to be auspicious if the water is gently trickling towards the house, symbolizing wealth rolling in. Trickling from the east and towards our beneficial direction is also auspicious.

We are at present in a period when it is considered auspicious to place a water feature in the east to signify good luck and wealth until 2003. From 2004 until 2023, the south-west will be considered auspicious.

There are many types of water feature available commercially and many more which could be created by an imaginative gardener. Whichever feature we choose should be in harmony with the surroundings in terms of design and materials and the elements around it should be balanced.

GARDEN FURNITURE AND STRUCTURES

As we expand our living space outside, the furnishings we choose should reflect the intended functions of the garden – play, entertainment, relaxation – as well as personal preferences. We should employ the same principles in our gardens as we do in our homes and carefully select furnishings that meet the purpose, reflect our tastes and support us.

▲ *An octagonal table is auspicious and allows everyone to communicate.*

► *A supportive shape, this chair looks like a very inviting place to sit and dream.*

Chairs and Tables

Garden chairs should follow the classic Four Animals formation and provide firm support for our backs as well as having arm rests. The colours chosen can be dictated by our individual preferences, but only if the Five Elements are taken into account. Chairs should be comfortable but as they are usually made of wood or metal they tend to be hard, which is acceptable if the design is right but uncomfortable if they are not ergonomically correct.

Tables should be chosen according to their function. Square tables are containing and a small square table by our favourite chair in a quiet spot may tend to keep us there and prevent us from searching for things to do. Round tables make for lively discussion but do not contain people for long. Rectangular tables with rounded ends are a common shape for garden furniture and are useful for summer lunch parties, although those seated at either end may sometimes feel left out. Octagonal tables are excellent because they are an auspicious shape and each person can communicate with everyone else around the table.

▼ *A perfect seat, circles and squares, with the four protective animal positions in place.*

▼ *A comfortable chair in which to spend a leisurely afternoon in the garden.*

Barbecues

Choosing a good location for a barbecue is mainly a matter of common sense. The north-west of the garden, next to a neighbour's fence where the south-west wind blows the smoke straight towards their kitchen window, is not a sensible choice. Barbecues are often positioned near a wall, but it is far better to position the cooking grid where the cook faces into the patio or terrace and is able to join in the party. Green is the best colour for a portable barbecue as black and blue represent the Water element and red might just add too much fuel to the flames.

Garden Buildings and Structures

Our gardens can also be furnished with buildings. Where we position these will affect their use and make a great impact on the overall structure and harmony of the garden. The materials used should blend with the surrounding buildings and the shapes and colours are important if we aim to keep a balance of yin and yang with the Five Elements.

▼ *A wonderful children's tree house that also blends well with its environment.*

▲ *The structures we build should blend in with the character of the garden.*

It is important that the house sits well in its environment and that we create stability at the four "cornerstones" of the garden – south-east, south-west, north-west and north-east. Garden buildings and decorative structures are a useful way of achieving this, provided they follow the Five Elements balance.

Where we use garden buildings for a specific purpose, such as our work, for growing seeds, or craft activities, the work bench should face one of our best directions, as determined earlier. We should arrange the layout to ensure that we face the entrance when standing at the bench. If this is not possible, then we should take measures to ensure we are not surprised from behind. A wind chime will alert us to someone entering and something reflective on the bench will enable us to see behind us. Mirrors are not recommended because the combination of mirror and sun can start a fire.

Some garden buildings are purely for decoration. Gazebos, although attractive to look at, are not comfortable to sit in as they are open to the wind. Structures with open sides offer no support when sitting and are therefore not ideal places in which to relax. Carefully positioned, however, they can provide excellent private spaces where we can escape and enjoy the solitude. Facing east, a gazebo can be a good place to eat an early breakfast and enjoy the energizing impact of the rising sun. Facing west, a gazebo will provide a restful spot to relax and unwind at the end of the day.

When siting garden features, take care that the edges and corners do not shoot "poison arrows" at the house or seating areas. Where points exist, climbing plants will soften or conceal them.

Useful Shapes and Colours for Cornerstones

Directions	Shapes		Colours
South-east			Brown, Green
South-west			Brown, Red
North-west			White, Silver, Brown
North-east		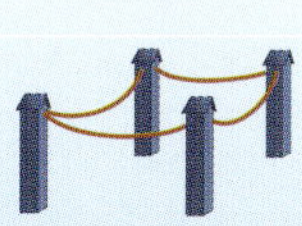	Brown, Blue

POTS AND ORNAMENTS

Containers of every conceivable size, colour and pattern are now available commercially, and they can be used to hold plants or as features on their own. Clay is the traditional material for pots and certainly plants look their best in them. Some pots are brightly coloured, which makes a welcome change and can look attractive, but they may clash with the natural colours in a garden. Consult the Five Elements table to check if the colours of the pots are compatible with the plants which will go in them. Shapes are also important and again the elements should be balanced.

Pots are imported from around the world, including many countries where frost is not a problem, so it is worth making sure that pots are frost-resistant if they are to stay outside during winter in colder climates. Frost may not be a problem when the pots are empty as it is the freezing and swelling of the water in the soil which causes pots to fracture. If plants are to remain outside in pots during the winter an extra-deep layer of drainage materials should be placed in the bottom at planting time and, when in position, the pots should be raised off the ground.

▲ *Pots of bulbs are useful throughout the year for a statement of colour. This one enlivens a dark corner.*

▲ *There is nothing dull about these pots of auriculas. They should be placed in a corner that needs bringing to life.*

Be aware of the impact the pots make. Highly decorative pots are generally suitable for formal gardens where they can be viewed from a distance but they may look out of place, or be an unnecessary expense, in a smaller garden, where they might be screened by other pots or where we will be looking down at them. We rarely notice pots at ground level and tend only to see the plants. Pots which are raised up are more noticeable.

Ornaments

Ornaments in the garden can be fun, particularly if they have been made by the owner. A garden can be a place in which to display our creativity and provides a wonderful backdrop for arts and crafts. Willow figures and wire sculptures are very popular and they have flowing lines which can bring a garden to life. Mosaics may be used as decorative features on pots and set into patios, pools and walls to bring vibrant colours into the garden. Stained glass is being increasingly used in windows and walls. Sundials are popular in gardens and can provide a useful learning aid for children.

▶ *Fire planting – use these colours to make a statement in the south or focus on Wealth in the south-east.*

◀ *Muscari never fail to please and are a welcome sight in Spring.*

▲ *A lovely corner in which to enjoy the fruits of our labours. Even a small town garden can have a similar restful space.*

▼ *Place animal ornaments with care so that they are in natural positions and with a background of the correct scale.*

Placing Pots and Ornaments

EAST: Wooden objects. Avoid metal, including wind chimes, and any pointed objects.
◆ Green and blue pots.

SOUTH: Wooden objects. Sundials.
◆ Green and red pots. Terracotta is included because of its reddish colour.

WEST: Terracotta or metal pots and ornaments.
◆ White or terracotta pots.

NORTH: Metal ornaments. Avoid terracotta and wood.
◆ White or blue pots.

▲ *A spotless cherub in a beautifully maintained garden.*

▼ *Use discarded items from the home to make unusual garden features*

Think about how an ornament will look in its garden setting: is it reassuring or will its shape cause you to jump as it looms out of a mist or at dusk? Only choose images you like.

Objects placed in the garden should blend in with the overall design. We should be able to observe them one at a time rather than all at once, which can confuse the eye. A single object at the end of a path will have a completely different effect to one which we happen to notice at a turn in the path. We should choose objects for the former position very carefully if we are not to be disappointed at the end of our journey.

▲ *With some imagination you can create unusual and original garden ornaments.*

▼ *Be sure to position sundials where they will receive the sun all day long.*

STATUES

Garden suppliers offer an excellent array of statuary, making it possible to create anything from an historical garden to a Japanese garden or even a fantasy garden full of fairies. The same design principles apply to statues as to any other aspect of Feng Shui. It is a question of proportion, style and materials and whether they blend with their surroundings. Another consideration is the impact they make on us subconsciously in a positive or negative sense.

Statues usually take the form of people or animals and we need to feel comfortable with the images we have in our gardens: we need to like the faces of the people they portray. Statues of small children can be pleasing, but may make us feel sad if our own children have grown up and left home, or if we are unable to have children. Statues of animals may be fun so long as they do not become a constant reminder of pets that have died, or resemble species we dislike. Be aware of a statue's energy, whether it is grim and dour or pert and lively, it will affect how we feel in the garden.

▲ *A beautiful delicate statue that is perfectly framed by the well-balanced planting.*

▼ *Friend or foe? This magnificent beast could prove frightening at dusk.*

▶ *New garden statuary may take time to become weathered and antique-looking.*

Statues are made from a variety of materials and they should blend in with and not stand out from their surroundings. Unblemished grey concrete is not aesthetically pleasant until it has aged and weathered. Fake verdigris on modern metal statues clashes with the natural greens of the plants in the garden. Brilliantly white statues have a harsh appearance and do not age well.

The placement of statues is important and ideally we should happen upon them as we take a meandering route around the garden, but they should not appear to leap out at us as we round a bend. It is not a good idea to place the life-size statue of a person in an open space as the effect can be disconcerting at night. Proportion is also important and bigger is not always better. A huge, ornately carved fountain sits well in Versailles but not in a small urban garden.

GARDEN LIGHTING

▲ *Candlelight and the floodlights under this tree create a romantic setting.*

There are two types of lighting in the garden. The first is practical, to enable us to make use of our gardens after dark, and the second is for special effects.

Lighting the Way

Particularly where there is no street lighting, it is important for occupants and visitors to gain safe access to the house.

◀ *Simple but effective – this lantern can prolong the time spent outdoors.*

Lights which line a path and those which are set into stair risers can make a homecoming much more welcoming than if we have to carefully pick our way through obstacles in the dark. One neglected area is the house name and number. How much more sociable for guests to be able to locate the house, the doorbell and, in the case of apartment buildings, the person's name. Floodlights are widely used, but ensure they are correctly positioned so that they are not triggered by every passing cat.

Garden lighting can extend the day. The key rule for lighting the garden is to keep it simple by accenting certain features to create a calm, yin atmosphere. Lighting placed below or nearby can light up a statue or rock and give it an entirely different night-time appearance.

Lighting up Plants

We normally view plants from above, but placing lights behind and under them enables us to view them from a different perspective and the results can be stunning. Trees lit from below, particularly blossom trees and those with interestingly shaped branches, can make wonderful features. Placing low-voltage lights in trees creates dancing shadows below as the light is filtered through the branches. Tiny bulbs in a tree produce an energetic party feel.

Garden lighting is best placed below eye level to reduce dazzle and to avoid creating shadows which can be disconcerting at night. We should aim to create pools of light that lead us through the garden rather than attempt to light up the whole area. Careful attention should be paid to siting the lights or we may experience feelings of unease as we peer into the dark spaces beyond.

Safety is paramount when we use electricity in the garden. Ponds should not contain lights, though perimeter lights can be stunning.

▶ *The lights in this modern town garden also make interesting shapes by day.*

CREATING THE GARDEN

With some knowledge of the principles behind Feng Shui, we will approach the creation of our gardens with a keener eye for detail. The plants we use – their colour, form, textures and smells – can feed our senses and create life-enhancing environments in which we can relax, entertain and indulge in our hobbies. Whether we have a minute basement or a rambling country garden, we can design our surroundings to support and nourish our senses.

THE HEALTHY GARDEN

A healthy garden is a place where we, the plants, and any food that we grow will thrive. Some plants are poisonous while others can adversely affect our health. Some gardening methods do not benefit us or the plants in the long term. There are alternatives to using chemicals in the garden, and our health and that of the wildlife will benefit if we turn to them where possible. If we follow the natural order then we, the plants, and the wildlife in the garden can live in harmony and support each other.

▲ *With careful planting we can obviate the need to use chemicals in the garden since nature can do the job just as well if we let it.*

POISONOUS PLANTS

Many well-known garden plants are poisonous and some wild ones may also find their way in. While adults are comparatively safe with these plants, children may be attracted by their colourful berries and seeds, and we need to take preventative measures to exclude dangerous plants from the garden at least when young children are part of the household.

POISONOUS GARDEN PLANTS

Laburnum, Lupins, Yew, Daphne

COMMON POISONOUS WILD PLANTS

Lords and ladies, Deadly nightshade, Black nightshade, Buckthorn

PLANTS AND ALLERGIES

In recent years there has been an increase in the number of people suffering from allergies. We regard the garden as a healthy place, but some of the plants we love best can cause a great deal of distress for asthma and hay fever sufferers and a number of plants can cause dermatitis when handled. Some popular plants which cause allergic reactions are shown in the box (right). Common names have been used as these plants are familiar to most people, even if they are not gardeners.

COMMON ALLERGENS

THE POLLEN OF: Grasses, Yarrow, Marigold
THE LEAVES OF: Chamomile, Ivy, Rue
THE SAP OF: Spurge, Christmas rose, Burning bush
THE SCENT OF: Pelargonium, Carnation (below), Evening primrose

MUTUAL SUPPORT

In nature there are few devastating plant diseases, nor are many plants wiped out by insect damage. This is because plants regulate themselves and a variety of plants grow together in a mutually supportive way. Some species secrete chemicals that are required by neighbouring plants, or which repel predators. Others provide shade for their neighbours. By far the most natural way to plant a garden is to grow trees, shrubs and perennial plants which will build up a relationship with each other and the earth. Annual plants and vegetables can fill the gaps. The soil is fed with compost made from prunings,

▲ *Grow herbs in containers, with other herbs, or in the herbaceous border.*

Herb Companions

Herb	Supports
Basil	Tomatoes
Borage	Strawberries
Chives	Apples
Garlic	Roses
Parsley	Asparagus
Tansy	Raspberries

leaves and kitchen waste, so it is in effect recycled from the garden itself. By bringing in outside composts (soil mix) and chemicals we create an imbalance and potential problems. If we follow the example of nature we will not dig the soil because this damages its structure and disturbs the creatures which work there for us, breaking down the organic matter. Some plants are known to be particularly beneficial to other plants growing close by. Many herbs fall into this category.

Plants to Deter Pests

In a healthy garden chemical-based formulas should not used to control insect pests because in doing so we may kill beneficial insects as well as the birds and small mammals which feed on them. Plants that are grown monoculturally are more vulnerable to insect damage than they would be if they were grown together with plants of other species. We can help this natural process further by introducing plants which secrete substances to repel certain types of pest.

Plants to Attract Predators

There are some insects which we should positively encourage into the garden, since they are predators of common garden pests. Certain plants act as hosts to these beneficial insects.

Pest Deterrents

Aphids: Fennel, nasturtiums, dill
Flea beetles: Catnip, hyssop, tomatoes
Colorado beetles: Coriander, onion, dandelion
Nematodes: African and French marigolds (below), chrysanthemums

Sacrificial Plants

We can also use plants to attract pests away from those we want to protect.

Mustard: Wireworms
Tobacco plant: Whitefly
Broad beans: Red spider mites
Nasturtiums: Blackfly

Plants to Attract Beneficial Predators

Wasps: Celery, chamomile, sunflowers
Hoverflies: Fennel, solidago, ivy
Ladybirds: Stinging nettles, tansy, yarrow

CHOOSING PLANTS

The rules for planting in the Feng Shui garden are simple. Each plant should be chosen carefully with regard to the specific features we wish to introduce. You need to think in terms of the colour, size and form of each individual plant, and how they will look side by side.

The planting should also blend in with the topography of the surrounding area – unless we want to make a definite statement to the contrary. You might live in an area that has identical houses in gardens which have evolved a particular look. You may feel happiest following the established style of your area, but since change is a key feature of Taoism, in which Feng Shui has its roots, individual expression in garden design is to be welcomed or we will not develop. When planting, the needs of plants should be taken into consideration in terms of soil type, aspect, temperature and spacing. There is no point attempting to nurture a plant which needs alkaline soil and a southerly aspect in a space that has acid soil, facing north. There will be less difficulty and disappointment in the garden

Favourite Seasonal Plants in China

Spring: Magnolia and Peony
Summer: Myrtle and Locust
Autumn: Maple and Chrysanthemum
Winter: Bamboo (below) and Wintersweet

◀ *Native plants flourish in a medieval-style English garden. Indigenous species will always grow better than imported plants in the right conditions.*

▲ *Plants need the correct soil and growing conditions in which to thrive.*

▼ *Summer in the garden – roses and lavender make good companion plants.*

Planting for Visual Impact

Flowers: Camellia, Magnolia, Orchid, Peony, Forsythia

Fruits: Crab-apple, Quince, Fig, Plum

Leaves: Weeping Willow, Maple, Palm, Privet

Seeds: *Clematis tangutica,* Physalis, Everlasting Pea, Eryngium (below)

▲ *Spruce trees should be planted alone.*

if plants are chosen wisely. Plants which are indigenous to an area will always grow best, since all the conditions will be right for them.

The Seasons

Gardens should have all-year-round interest and, more importantly, we should be able to see the changes brought about by the seasons through windows from inside the house and also from various vantage points in the garden.

Within each season it is considered desirable that each stage of a plant's development should be represented – flowers, leaves, fruits and seed.

Trees

Trees are used to enhance a space, to obscure unwelcome features and to balance other features in the garden. In ancient China, trees were regarded as having special powers. We are more aware now of the importance to our ecological system of trees and the way in which they act as the lungs of the planet.

Trees need to be planted meticulously to reflect a number of philosophical principles as follows:

◆ Trees should grow naturally, since their beauty is in their true shape.

◆ A single tree can be admired for its shape, bark, leaves and blossom.

◆ Groups of trees should be in odd numbers; threes or fives.

◆ Trees with branches growing horizontally, such as cedar or spruce, should be planted alone.

◆ Upright trees, such as bamboo or cypress, should not be planted alongside trees with horizontal branches.

◆ Weeping and pendulous trees, like willow or birch, do not mix with those bearing horizontal branches.

◆ Only trees with a canopy, such as oak or elm, are suitable for mass planting.

◆ Trees with distinctive shapes, such as yew and plane, should be planted alone.

▼ *The deeply furrowed trunk of the Dawn redwood. The bark of a tree can be as beautiful and remarkable as any flower.*

GARDENING FOR THE SENSES

We respond to our gardens through our emotions and senses. The scent of a favourite plant can bring on a feeling of euphoria, while stroking the hairy leaves of *Stachys lanata*, or lambs' ears, can be soothing.

SIGHT

When we think of sight it is usually in terms of the immediate visual impression made by a tree or a flower bed and whether or not we like what we see. In the Feng Shui garden, seeing is rather more than that. When we look at a tree we should see the shape of its trunk, observe the way the branches spread out and the intricate criss-crossing of the canopy. We should also perceive the veining on the leaves and the patterning on the bark and notice the small creatures busying themselves on it. We may think that it resembles an old man, slightly stooped, as it is highlighted against the glowing red of the evening sky. If we let our imagination run riot, he may appear to be wearing Aunt Hilda's sun hat with the large bunch of cherries on the side and if we were then to call the scene "Grandfather wearing Aunt Hilda's hat", we would be coming close to the way the Chinese perceive the world in their art and philosophy.

▼ *The magnificent show of colour provided by this Cotinus* obovatus *will encourage anyone to plant it for seasonal interest.*

▲ *There is immediate visual interest in this busy garden, but a single flower could make just as powerful a statement.*

Observing the seasons is important in the Feng Shui garden, and we should plant carefully to ensure that we maintain some interest all the year round. We can achieve this by:

- Arranging plants which have different flowering times in tiers.
- Positioning flowers of the same colour but with different flowering periods in successive tiers.
- Mixing plants which have different flowering times.
- Planting varieties with long flowering times and vivid colours.
- Planting trees first and filling the gaps with perennials.

What we see when we look out into our gardens is of the utmost importance, not only for the pleasure it gives us, but because of the subconscious impression it makes on us, which can affect us psychologically. Clutter around the garden, just as it is inside the house, will become a constant source of irritation.

WINTER INTEREST IN THE GARDEN

FOLIAGE PLANTS

Cornus alba, Vitis vinifera 'Purpurea', *Liquidambar styraciflua*

FLOWERING PLANTS

Hamamelis x *intermedia* 'Pallida', *Jasminum nudiflorum, Viburnum* x *bodnantense, Choisya ternata*

BERRIES

Cotoneaster horizontalis, Skimmia, Pyracantha (below), Holly

BARK

Acer capillipes, Pinus pinea, Prunus serrula

▲ *We can rely on wildlife or create our own sounds in the garden. This bamboo wind chime will resound gently in the breeze.*

Sound

It is rare in the modern world to be able to escape from the noise of machinery or traffic, even in the garden, although by planting trees and dense hedges we can cushion ourselves to a certain extent. The garden itself is not really silent, and we would wish to encourage the sounds of nature there. Birdsong is always welcome, except perhaps for the harsh cawing of crows or the repetitive cooing of pigeons. Through careful planting, we can encourage the small songbirds into the garden, by tempting them with berries, seeds and the small insects which will be there if we do not spray with chemicals. The buzzing of bees while they work is another welcome noise which we can foster by adding their favourite plants.

The sound of gurgling water is relaxing, and bamboo plants, willow trees and tall grasses all make gentle swishing noises in the breeze. Placing Aeolian harps and wooden or shell wind chimes near where we sit is a good idea, provided we keep them near the house so they do not interfere with the finely tuned hearing of the wildlife. In the early autumn we should not be in too much of a hurry to sweep up since children like nothing more than the simple pleasure of crunching through leaves.

Clutter

Unwashed flower pots
Leaves in corners
Plants which catch on our clothes
Plants which catch our ankles
Dead branches
Dead plants
Overgrown hedges
Any jobs left undone

Case Study

Even a garden in a perfect setting requires careful planning. Harry and Ann had a back garden with a beautiful view but when they hired a garden designer they did not feel comfortable with the result. A Feng Shui consultant came up with the following solution.

This beautiful open garden has a river meandering along the bottom and hugging the house. In the Phoenix position is a large oak tree marking the boundary of the property and beyond that a wonderful meadow with wild flowers, where horses graze.

The designer incorporated a row of conifers from the river to the door, blocking the wide view and creating a "poison arrow" of harmful chi from the gnarled trunk of the oak, which had become a threat to the house. This was likely to make the people living in the house feel irritable and restricted. At worst, this could result in mental instability and put a strain on their marriage. Removing the conifers from the design enabled Harry and Ann to have the full benefit of the wonderful view from their house once more.

► *Bamboo is an integral part of Chinese gardens, art and culture and grows well in a Western gravel garden.*

Touch

Touch is a sense which is often neglected in the garden. We tend to venture forth with caution, wearing gardening gloves and alerted to the perils lurking in the soil, the chemicals we have sprayed on the leaves, and even the plants themselves. Certainly we should be aware of the dangers, but to forgo the pleasure of feeling the soil running through our fingers as we plant a precious seedling, of burying our faces in a conifer after rain to smell its heady resinous scent, or to run our hands over rosemary and lavender as we pass, is to lose our connection with the earth.

The leaves of plants provide a range of sensations – stroking the woolly leaves of verbascum, the cold smooth leaves of mesembryanthemums or the rough carpet of dwarf thyme each gives its own form of tactile pleasure. The texture of bark on trees ranges from perfectly smooth to the peeling bark of the paper birch. We can get pleasure from stroking the soft petals of an iris or lily, or the face of a sunflower, or running our hands over the surface of the grass.

▲ *When harvesting your own fruit and vegetables remember to enjoy the feel of the earth and its produce.*

Taste

Nothing tastes better than home-grown fruit and vegetables, and it is possible to

▲ *No shop-bought produce can beat the taste of home-grown vegetables freshly dug from the garden.*

◀ *Rosemary delights in many ways – the colour of the flowers, the bees it attracts and the feel and smell of its leathery foliage.*

▶ *Fruit does not have to take up a lot of space: cordons or espaliers grown on walls and fences can be very productive.*

Scented plants

Spring

Daphne odora, Viburnum fragrans, Osmanthus burkwoodii, Ribes odoratum

Summer

Deutzia, Philadelphus, *Cytisus battandieri, Lupinus aboreus*

Autumn

Lonicera fragrantissima, Rosemary, Lavender, Sage

Winter

Chimonanthus praecox, Sarcococca hookeriana digyna, Hamamelis mollis, Acacia dealbata

▼ *The herb garden below will be full of wonderful aromas.*

grow them in the smallest of spaces. Salad vegetables sown in succession in a border will feed us through the summer months. Fruit trees grown on dwarfing rootstocks take up little space. Those grown on a single upright stem can be grown in pots near where we sit, to give us pleasure and remind us of earth's bounty. The taste of a freshly-picked sun-warmed apple or of tomatoes plucked from the vine in passing takes some beating. Herb beds close to the house also offer tempting flavours and lemon balm, sorrel, chervil, basil and parsley can give us a wide range of taste experiences.

▼ *A traditional wattle fence provides the backdrop for this mixed herb bed.*

Smell

No manufactured perfume surpasses the smell of a damask rose or of wild honeysuckle. The joy of scent in the garden is its subtlety. When the smell of elderflowers fills the house on a damp evening we crave more, but that would mask the other smells which drift in from the garden. The scents of *Lilium regale* and wintersweet are pervasive. Others will need to be placed near paths where we can brush against them to release the fragrance of plants like *Choisya ternata* and eucalyptus. Some plants do not object to being trodden on occasionally, and the Treneague chamomile and most thymes are suitable for planting on or near to paths.

▲ *Roses, particularly the old-fashioned varieties, provide a heady perfume.*

▼ *Some lilies are very fragrant and a pot by the back door will scent the kitchen.*

COLOUR

▲ *Our response to colour in the garden is emotional and psychological.*

We all respond to colour in different ways, as is evident in the way we dress and decorate our homes. Our response is emotional and psychological and sometimes colours which we do not like can even bring about a physical response. In the Feng Shui garden, colour is part of the way in which the planting fits in with the garden's immediate environment, and with the natural contours of the landscape. In the natural world, colour blends into the background hue of the place – green in woodland, sand and pebble colours on the coast, purple shades on mountain slopes. If we look at poppies in a field they appear to shimmer on the surface,whereas a formal planting of marigolds or salvias in a park forms a solid mass of colour.

The way in which we group plants is a matter of taste but all too often it is a hit-or-miss affair. If we examine an artist's use of colour, it can give us clues as to the harmonies which exist between different colours.

When any two of the three basic colours, red, blue and yellow, are mixed they give rise to a secondary colour – orange, violet, or green. These six colours make up the basic colour wheel as adapted by Gertrude Jekyll, whose harmonious planting ideas have influenced

◀ *Observe the impact of the poppies which appear to shimmer across the field behind.*

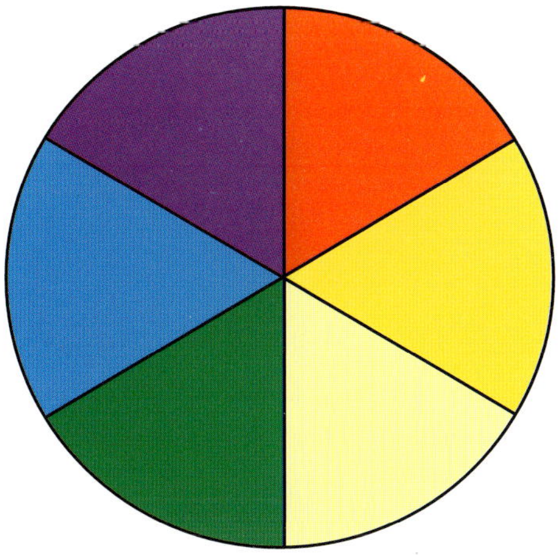

▲ *Use this simple diagrammatic colour wheel as a guide to basic colour harmonies and contrasts.*

gardeners all over the world. Three adjacent colours are known as harmonies. The others are contrasts. Those which sit diagonally opposite are complementary. Most of us respond positively to colours which are in harmony, and either complement or contrast with one another. In places where these rules cannot be applied, conflicting colours should be separated by neutral ones – white, grey or dark green.

In recent years research has been conducted into the use of colour in healing. Feng Shui practitioners believe that it is possible to determine a person's health or mood by the colours they use in their environment and that it is possible to alter perceptions by changing colours or by combining them in a variety of ways. It is fun to experiment and create gardens in which the colours are supportive and inspirational. Colours affect our mood, and it is worth remembering this when planning a garden in any climate.

Colour is affected by the quality of the light. In Morocco and the Mediterranean countries bright colours look magnificent: brilliant red pelargoniums in Spanish courtyards are a sight to behold. Larger civic gardens and parks in these countries use green and abundant foliage to create cool shade, and a feeling of oasis-like sanctuary from the heat.

▲ *White breaks up the vivid pink and orange plants in this bed.*

◀ *A stunning colour for a Mediterranean garden. The tone would need to be adjusted for it to work in a cooler climate.*

▼ *Vivid colours work well in hot countries because of the quality of the sunlight.*

PLANTING WITH A COLOUR THEME

We have seen that colour alters our emotions and moods, but we can also use colour to focus on areas of the Bagua, depending on the elemental qualities of the area.

Red

Red plants will dominate a garden when planted in large patches and are not restful to sit near. They make excellent spot plants to draw the eye to a certain area.

▲ *Red plants like this* Euonymus alatus *'Compactus' make an impact at a distance.*

RED TREES AND SHRUBS: *Acer rubrum, Berberis thunbergii* 'Atropurpurea', *Cotinus coggygria, Euonymus alatus* 'Compactus'.
RED HERBACEOUS PLANTS: *Ajuga reptans, Bergenia cordifolia, Paeonia lactiflora.*

White and Silver

All-white gardens appear fresh and clean and, in the evening light, luminous. Although calming, there may be a deadness to a large all-white garden unless it is carefully planned with many different shades and shapes of green to vary it.
WHITE TREES AND SHRUBS: *Pyrus salicifolia, Drimys winteri, Skimmia japonica* 'Fructu Albo'.
WHITE HERBACEOUS PLANTS: *Eremurus himalaicus, Aruncus dioicus, Astilbe* 'Irrlicht'.

Yellow

Yellow is usually associated with spring and late summer. It is a rich and cheerful colour, but, in its paler forms or when combined with white, it can feel uncomfortable and demoralizing.

◀ *White in a garden can soothe but also be strangely lifeless with no other colours near.*

▲ *Yellow works well in this understated mixed planting.*

▼ *A collection of hostas showing just how many shades of green there are.*

YELLOW TREES AND SHRUBS: *Laburnum x watereri* 'Vossii', *Acer japonicum* 'Aureum', *Hypericum* 'Hidcote'.
YELLOW HERBACEOUS PLANTS: *Phlomis russeliana, Rudbeckia fulgida* 'Goldsturm', *Achillea filipendulina* 'Gold Plate'.

Green

Spot planting, using pots of coloured plants and bulbs, is very effective against the backdrop of a green garden. In itself, the green garden, containing various shades and shapes of foliage, can be a

▲ *Muscari brings this gravel garden to life.*

restful, tranquil place. Green is the predominant colour in the Chinese garden.

GREEN TREES AND SHRUBS: *Juniperus chinensis, Chamaecyparis lawsoniana, Thuja occidentalis.*

GREEN HERBACEOUS PLANTS: Hostas, *Phyllostachys nigra,* Euphorbia.

BLUE

Blue borders have a sedative effect but unrelieved blue can be gloomy. Blue plants can be mixed with white and silver foliage and with soft pink flowers.

BLUE TREES AND SHRUBS: *Picea glauca* 'Coerulea', *Ceanothus impressus, Abies concolor* 'Glauca Campacta'.

BLUE HERBACEOUS PLANTS: *Echinops bannaticus, Gentiana asclepiadea, Salvia patens.*

PURPLE

A purple border can be sumptuous and restful at the same time. Mix purple with blues, whites and soft pinks for calm.

PURPLE TREES AND SHRUBS: *Jacaranda mimosifolia,* Syringa, *Hydrangea macrophylla.*

▼ *Purple and red make a powerful combination in this tub.*

▲ *Pink is a warm colour. This pink works remarkably well with the black pansies.*

PURPLE HERBACEOUS PLANTS: *Verbena patagonica,* Iris, *Salvia nemorosa* 'May Night'.

PINK

Pink is a warm colour and draws people to it. The gentler shades are preferable.

PINK TREES AND SHRUBS: *Magnolia campbellii,* Prunus, Spiraea.

PINK HERBACEOUS PLANTS: Lavatera, Peony, Geranium.

ORANGE

Orange is a rich, warm, happy colour, but difficult to place. It is probably best against a dark green background.

ORANGE TREES AND SHRUBS: *Spathodea campanulata,* Berberis, *Leonotis leonurus.*

ORANGE HERBACEOUS PLANTS: Rudbeckia, *Lychnis chalcedonica,* Chrysanthemum.

▼ *The colours work well together here since the shades are subtle and not harsh.*

THE COURTYARD GARDEN

Depending on the style of the property, courtyard gardens can be formal or great fun, giving expression to the artistic talent latent in everyone. With walls or fences to paint, floor surfaces to experiment with and only a tiny space to fill, courtyards can allow us unlimited scope for expression.

Often the difficulty in designing a small garden is in deciding what not to include. Gardens packed full of plants, using several different materials and textures, can appear fussy and make the space look even smaller than it is. On the other hand, the impact of one architectural plant with some pebbles and moss can look stunning in a tiny space, although gardens which are too minimal emphasize their small size.

▲ *Careful planting at a variety of levels creates a haven of peace and beauty in a tiny courtyard.*

► *A restrained use of colour stops a small space from looking too fussy.*

A wide variety of materials is available now and, cleverly combined, they can become a work of art in themselves. Beware of surfaces which are likely to become slippery in damp areas: decking can look stunning when sun-baked by a pool, but in a dark shady area it can become stained and unpleasant. Often such spaces create their own microclimate where we can grow plants which will not normally grow outside. If a courtyard is overlooked, overhead wires supporting a vine will afford privacy while letting in light, creating an exotic Mediterranean feeling in the middle of a town.

Every feature in a small garden needs to earn its keep and it is self-defeating to hold on to a plant which has outgrown

◄ *Wall-mounted pelargoniums are common in Mediterranean courtyards.*

Architectural Plants for Impact

Cordyline australis, Acer, *Fatsia japonica*, Fatshedera, *Juniperus scopulorum*, Box (below)

Plants for Shade

Euonymus fortunei 'Silver Queen', *Choisya ternata*, Philadelphus, Skimmia

Plants to Hide Walls

Campsis radicans, *Actinidia kolomikta*, Ivy, Jasmine, Roses (below)

its space or is past its prime. It constitutes clutter if it is a problem. We need to make the best use of trees and interesting features outside our own gardens and borrow them for our own design. Those we do not want – ugly walls, unsightly pipes and other features – we can blot

▼ *Climbers and baskets can be useful where ground space is limited.*

Combinations of Materials

Wooden decking and pebbles
Shingle and granite slabs
Stone and moss
Coloured concrete and mosaics
Paving slabs and brick

out. Coloured trellis can work wonders on an unsightly wall. The plants we choose should be those which will fill the space when they reach maturity. They may take longer to grow than fast-growing species, but will ultimately be more rewarding since they will not cause maintenance problems later.

Some houses have enclosed spaces, with access only from a window, but if we design with care, we can use the colour and textures of different materials to create interesting and energetic spaces there. Some plants thrive in the most unlikely places. With just a chink of light in the darkest cave, a fern will usually grow, and the ivy family is invaluable in awkward corners. In small spaces, plants may even be incidental if we use materials, water and illusion to design what is essentially another room. Ornaments, sculptures and pots, strategically placed mirrors and brightly coloured walls can create stunning environments which will energize and stimulate us.

▼ *Strategically placed pots can enliven any space and are useful in paved courtyards.*

CASE STUDY

Moira and her family had just finished renovating an old house. Moira loved the spaciousness of their new home and the feeling that the family were doing things together, but she craved a space for herself where she could pursue her hobby – watercolour painting. The renovations had left a small courtyard at the back of the house.

1. The lean-to greenhouse was renovated to enable Moira to store her art materials and overwinter some plants.

2. The basement staircase was made safe by installing a gate. A trellis (Earth shape in the north-east) gave some height to the planting. A blue *Clematis alpina* scrambles over it.

3. Planting has been kept to a minimum so that watering does not become a chore, and because the space is small. Single plants, if they are large, can give a feeling of lusciousness and so a *Prunus stiloba simplex* was positioned here.

4. A cordyline was placed in this corner to liven it up and in front, a small pebble water feature was also added.

5. A terracotta wall feature of an upright jug was placed here to raise the view above the staircase and lifts the energy of the north-east.

6. Moira's chair and easel are here. A canopy above the window shields them when it is hot. Since the window leads into the house it was not felt to be a problem behind the chair.

7. This table and storage unit for Moira's painting equipment can be wheeled into the greenhouse.

8. An ivy covered ball brings a playful energy to this corner

9. Moira plans to have a mosaic wall here with a blank space above the table for her still life arrangements. The space opens up ideas from the rising energy of the east, which Moira can draw on from her position opposite.

10. Moira hopes to sell her paintings one day. Taking her chair as the mouth of chi, and aligning the symbolic Bagua with it, this wall is the Offspring area. Moira plans to paint murals on this wall, which she can change over the years.

ROOFS AND BASEMENTS

▲ *Wooden decking creates an indoor feel to this well designed outdoor space.*

In urban areas where space is at a premium, living areas extend upwards and downwards. For people living in the centre of a city, a roof garden is a haven from the bustling life below. For those who live below street level in basements, sometimes their only view is of walls and of feet passing overhead. Both these spaces are difficult when planning a garden. The roof garden is totally exposed and unsupported, with little chance of capturing chi unless some structural alterations are made. In the basement garden chi becomes trapped and stagnant since it cannot circulate, so careful planning and planting are needed.

▼ *This country cottage-style garden is actually on an urban roof.*

Roof Gardens

Roof gardens are unique in that they encompass a number of problems which are not found all in one place in a conventional garden. Structure and load-bearing capacity are the first priorities, followed by drainage.

High winds will be a problem. Open trellis is preferable to a solid screen which creates wind turbulence. Winds cause damage to young shoots and causes soil to dry out quickly so maintenance is high, watering systems are an advantage. A light gravel layer on top of the pots will help to conserve moisture. Light free-draining compost (soil mix) in the pots and containers is preferable to heavy garden soil. Feeding will be necessary.

Temperatures may be higher than average in big citites. Pergolas can be used for shading, but great care should be taken that the structures are secure. Overhead wires are another option.

In such an unnatural environment plants will eventually outgrow their space and the only option will be to replace them. Sickly plants create stagnant chi and should be renewed quickly. It is possible to grow vegetables and fruit on roofs, either in pots or in growing bags.

▲ *On this secluded roof you would never dream you were in the city.*

▼ *Quarry tiles can be a hard-wearing and practical surface for a roof garden.*

Plants for Roof Gardens

Climbers

Clematis alpina, Hedera helix, Passiflora

Trees

Rhus typhina 'Laciniata', Ficus, *Acer negundo*

Architectural plants

Cordyline, Magnolia (below), Salix

Shrubs

Hebe, Lavender, Santolina

Herbs

Parsley, Basil, Chives

Vegetables

Tomato, Asparagus pea, Salad vegetables

Lighting is a consideration on the roof since there may not be sufficient light generated from within the building. Uplighters are useful since they show off the plants but avoid causing glare which could disturb neighbours.

Basements

At the other end of the scale, basements can be confined places with restricted amounts of natural light available. However, these conditions can be alleviated. If the outlook from the windows is bleak and the basement area is damp and fills up with wind-blown rubbish and leaves it is important to summon up the energy and initiative to clear up and take control of the space. Living without much natural light can drain personal energy so, in the basement garden, the object is to raise the chi of the space and the spirits of the occupants.

▲ *This* trompe l'oeil *effect seems to double the perceived size of the basement area.*

▼ *This could have been a dismal basement area but it has been transformed by the addition of scores of potted plants.*

Light-coloured walls are essential in a basement, and dark walls should be painted white. If the walls are high use a trellis to support climbing plants, rooted in the ground, if possible, or in large pots. As the plants grow and climb upwards they will raise the energy. Choose plants which are evergreen or have fairly large leaves, or clearing up will be a problem. Lush simplicity is preferable to fussy planting where space is restricted.

If there are stairs which are wide enough, pots of colourful plants can be placed at intervals to light the way. Avoid trailing plants, like ivy, which will have a depressing effect. Gertrude Jekyll suggested that even in the smallest space there should be a distinctive feature – an ornament, fountain or raised bed to create an interesting focal point.

Lighting is important in basements, and uplighters, shining through climbing plants, can improve the energy. Visual illusion can be used to good effect with murals or *trompe l'oeil*, or even strategically placed mirrors, and the area can be cheered by a bright floor surface – tiles and mosaics can be used if they blend in with the surrounding architecture.

Plants for Basements

Shrubs

Fatsia japonica, Fatshedera, Arundinaria, Cornus

Climbers

Wisteria sinensis, Chaenomeles speciosa, Hydrangea petiolaris, Parthenocissus quinquefolia

Ferns

Dryopteris dilatata, Polypodium vulgare, Phyllitis scolopendrium, Polystichum aculeatum

TERRACES AND PATIOS

Terraces, or patio areas, feature in both urban and rural gardens. They can be as simple as a few rows of paving outside the back door, or elaborate balustraded affairs running the length of grand country houses. Whatever their size, they enable a range of activities to take place and the emphasis will change over time as children arrive, grow up and eventually leave home, when parents can return to a more leisurely lifestyle. With careful planning, paddling pools and sand pits can be transformed into flower beds.

The size of the terrace will be determined by the size of the garden and should be in proportion. Those less than 2m (6ft) wide do not really allow enough room for much activity to happen there. Privacy may be a problem. Depending on the direction the terrace faces, some protection from the wind may be needed. Overhead shading may be required in the form of a plant-covered pergola, giving a dappled light effect, or a canopy to give more complete cover.

Patios can become extremely yang places in the height of summer, with the sun blazing overhead, the hard surfaces giving off heat, pools and metal objects

▲ *A dream terrace in an idyllic situation where the planting complements the view.*

▼ *A shady retreat from the hot sun, this terrace blends in well with the house.*

▼ *Tomatoes grow well in pots and are ideally close for picking if grown on a terrace.*

and tables reflecting the glare. By introducing some height in the form of shading, and with plants around the edges as well as in containers, we can create a balance and make a cool and relaxing place to sit.

▲ *A delightful terrace with the view framed like a picture between the planting.*

▶ *Many fruit varieties are now grown on dwarf rootstocks suitable for growing in pots.*

Terraces need easy access from the kitchen if eating or entertaining is to take place there. In north-facing gardens it is advisable to place terraces at a distance from the house, where they will have some sun and can be reached via a hard path so that trolleys can be wheeled along and people can carry dishes safely. On small terraces, built-in seating will save space and can look attractive if the materials used blend into the overall plan and with the house. On the other hand, built-in seating with raised beds behind it can be uncomfortable if insects are attracted to the area by the plants. Often on terraces, chairs are not backed by a wall, so if we want to keep our guests there for any length of time, we should provide them with high-backed chairs.

If the terrace is used for reading or quiet reflection we should place our chairs to face one of our auspicious directions. We can also align sun-loungers in the same way, depending on which way the terrace faces.

A paved area or deck may be a large space that is required for a variety of different family activities. Young children may like to have a sand pit and paddling pool there, though if you do have both, it is a good idea to keep the two well apart. Be mindful of the Five Elements when positioning the paddling pool. It is advisable to cover both the sand pit and the pool when not in use, especially if you have cats that are fond of using the former as a litter tray. Covering the pool will ensure that the water remains clean and hygienic.

Small children may want to ride trikes in the garden, so the patio or deck should be level with the adjoining grass area to prevent accidents. Where the area is raised and there are steps, secure barriers should be erected. Swings should never be placed on hard surfaces; if they are not on grass, bark chippings or another soft surface should be placed underneath.

The area near the house may also need to accommodate a number of items such as dustbins (trash cans), wood piles, sheds and washing lines. Keep these separate from any seating, hidden behind plant-covered screens or fences if possible.

Plants for the Terrace

Climbers
Clematis, *Lathyrus grandiflorus*, Vitis, Gourds, Wisteria

Small Trees for Shade
Catalpa bignoniodes, *Corylus alternifolia* 'Argentea', Acer, Prunus, Magnolia

Plants to train on walls
Malus, Ceanothus, Pyracantha, Jasmine, Chaenomeles

Herbs for the Barbecue
Rosemary, Sage (below bottom), Thyme, Oregano (below top)

Fruit and Vegetables for Pots
Tomatoes, Peppers, Aubergines Strawberries (below), Apples

RURAL GARDENS

In the rural garden the possibilities for design would appear to be greater than in the urban garden. Yet, in many ways, the design is more restricted by convention and the need to blend in with the natural landscape. In the Feng Shui garden, we capture the landscape and draw it into our gardens while, at the same time, ensuring that the garden is an extension of the house, linked physically but also by style.

Boundaries in the rural garden can be hidden by planting linked into a hill or group of trees beyond, which we can frame and use as our own. We can create boundaries within the garden using trellis, gateways and gaps in hedges to lead our eyes on and suggest new experiences beyond. Even a closed door in a wall will suggest possibilities, and adds an air of mystery. Proportion is important and can make all the difference to the feel of a garden. Tall narrow openings are far less inviting than wide ones. Since rural gardens are often larger than their city counterparts, it will not always be necessary to disguise the boundary or block out an ugly view. Rather than planting at the edge, a tree in the lawn with space to move behind will add depth and more interest to the garden.

Within the plot we can create special areas: places to be alone, to entertain, for the children to play and so on, always bearing in mind that the elements need to be balanced with regard to colour and shapes and that we need to maintain a balance of yin and yang, combining hard landscaping with soft planting, and in the height of plants or the shapes of their leaves.

Paths should meander through the garden, opening up new vistas at each turn and allowing us to happen upon things such as statues, rocks, pots or prize plants. A path can take us directly to the shed or greenhouse, which should ideally be situated fairly near to the house for

◄ *The "rooms" in this medieval-style garden mimic field divisions in the landscape beyond and are in harmony with it.*

▲ *A few pots at the base of the tree act as a stop before the eye moves on to travel around the garden.*

◄ *A variety of heights, shapes, forms and colours in planting schemes will ensure that the yin-yang balance is maintained.*

▲ *Produce which is harvested once a year can be positioned at the end of the garden.*

◀ *The plants in this garden have built up a relationship with their environment.*

convenience, and from there to the vegetable patch or fruit-growing area. We may like to consider the possibility of cultivating crops which take longer to grow and take up a lot of space, or are harvested infrequently – such as potatoes, asparagus and rhubarb – at the bottom of the garden, and those which we need on a daily basis – like herbs and salad vegetables – near to the house. A path, or even stepping stones in the lawn to the vegetable garden, will enable us to pick produce even on the wettest day. Picking a lettuce is less fun if you need to find boots and wet weather gear first.

Water makes a difference in any garden, but remember that all the creatures in the garden and surrounding area will be attracted to it. If you are not willing to share your terrace with hundreds of baby frogs, a fox, mice and the odd visiting rat, site the pond away from the house and, if you stock it with fish, be prepared for herons.

We should allow plants to breathe by enabling the wind to blow through them; spacing them well will mean less disease. We should extend this principle, by opening up the centres of each area and enabling the chi to circulate and move on. Above all we should respect the spirit of the place and choose plants and materials which are at home there, remembering that there are many things which human beings have to learn about the natural world and that the less we tamper with it and poison it, the better it will be for us, our families and the generations to come.

Rural Garden Plants

Plants for Hedges
Aucuba, Berberis, Euonymus, Ribes, Ilex, Mahonia

Plants for Shady Places
Arundinaria, *Aucuba japonica*, *Fatsia japonica*, Eleagnus, Mahonia, Skimmia

Shrubs for Interest
Chaenomeles, Cotoneaster, Hebe, Philadelphus, Pyracantha, Viburnum

Ground Cover Plants
Ajuga reptans, Bergenia, *Euphorbia amygdaloides*, Helleborus, Hosta, *Hypericum calycinum*

Trees for Small Gardens
Acer, Betula, Eucalyptus, Malus, Prunus, Sorbus

Plants for Pool Sides
Astilbe, Hosta, Iris, Ranunculus, Rheum, Trollius

Scented Plants
Oenothera (below left), Lavender (below right), Jasmine, Honeysuckle

WATERSIDE GARDENS

Water, in the form of pools, waterfalls and streams, is an important element in the Feng Shui garden. When the garden is situated beside a large river or lake, or by the sea, its design needs some special consideration.

Coastal Gardens

Coastal gardens are among the most difficult to cultivate. The effects of the salt-laden winds can spread as far as 8km (5 miles) inland, bending plants and trees double and scorching the leaves. However, given some shelter, these can also be the most rewarding gardens since they are virtually frost-free and rarely have snow. The climate lends itself to growing many plants which will not grow elsewhere.

The quality of the light in coastal locations is more vibrant than it is inland and planting can be brighter, although very colourful planting can seem harsh on dull days. Seaside resorts in temperate northern climes can come alive in summer when brilliant pelargoniums grow against whitewashed walls and give a Mediterranean feel. In winter it is often

▼ *Bright Mediterranean colours – of plants and paint – look good in a seaside garden.*

▲ *Low planting is less likely to suffer wind damage than taller plants.*

a matter of battening down the hatches, and hanging baskets and pots have to be secured against the elements. There is no better illustration of yin and yang than the vibrant yang bustle of a summertime resort in contrast with the yin stillness of the calm sea in the bay. When the holidaymakers have departed in the winter, the resort becomes quiet and yin while the sea is churned up and becomes yang.

Beach gardens can be fun and look attractive adorned with driftwood and other items washed up by the sea. Few plants flourish in such locations, but some grasses and plants which grow naturally there, such as horned poppies and thrift, do well. Windbreaks should fit in with the look of the area and bamboo or rush permeable fencing will help to fend off the wind. There are a number of shrubs that are useful as hedging in such areas. Higher up are the cliff-side gardens

▲ *Many tropical plants will also grow in temperate conditions in protected locations.*

▼ *The results of beachcombing make a natural seaside garden.*

Plants for Coastal Gardens

Windbreaks

Atriplex, *Crataegus monogyna* 'Stricta', *Escallonia rubra, Griselinia littoralis*

Shrubs

Hebe, *Halimium libanotis, Tamarix ramosissima, Hippophae rhamnoides* – Sea Buckthorn

Rock Plants

Dianthus alpinus (below), *Pulsatilla vulgaris, Sedum spathulifolium, Sempervivum arachnoideum*

Plants to Try

Phormium tenax, Cordyline australis 'Atropurpurea', *Livistona chinensis, Dodonaea viscosa* 'Purpurea'

which fringe many coastal towns. Planted on the cliff face and linked by meandering paths, they escape the worst of the weather and can reveal some gems of plants, more suited to tropical climates.

Riverside Gardens

Riverside locations can be idyllic, particularly in summer. Homes bordering a river tend to be orientated towards it and occasionally the mouth of chi, the entrance, becomes the rear of the house. Fast-moving water is felt to dissipate energy and certainly the banks of fast-moving rivers are not home to the variety of plants which thrive by those which meander gently through the garden. Waterside gardens can incorporate a range of plants which do not thrive in other conditions: lush green carpets of bay arums provide a perfect foil for the dancing swards of sweet flag and the narrow stems of irises and rushes. Equally magnificent, delicate weeping willows vie for attention with the massive leaves of gunnera. It is not advisable to block the view of the river but to set a small shrub or rock as the boundary in the Phoenix position, and frame the river with some planting to block its coming and going at the boundaries – symbolic in China of wealth coming in then running away.

In urban and inner city areas, where heavy industry has moved out, housing developments often spring up around rivers and in dockland areas. Huge buildings dwarf most planting schemes and where possible, large trees should be introduced to create some yin energy.

▲ *This garden has incorporated the river as part of its design.*

▼ *A slow-moving river at the bottom of the garden can be auspicious.*

ACKNOWLEDGEMENTS

The publishers would like to thank the following picture libraries for the use of their pictures.
A-Z Botanical Collection Ltd.: 36tr(Jean Deval), br(Robert Murray); 48t(Bjorn Svensson); 62br(Margaret Higginson); 84tr(J. Whitworth); 93tr(A. Stenning), b(J. Whitworth). **Bruce Coleman**: 31bl; 32r(Paul van Gaalen), m (Stefano Amantini); 37r; 43bl(Dr.Stephen Coyne). **The Garden Picture Library**: 34-5(Ron Sutherland); 37tl(Erika Craddock); 39tr(Erika Craddock), bl(Juliette Wade), br(Erika Craddock); 40tr(Ron Sutherland), bl(Ron Sutherland); 41tr; 42tr(John Glover); 52tr(Eric Crichton); 56-7; 60bl; 63br(Steven Wooster); 69tl(Ron Sutherland), bl(Sunniva Harte), br(John Glover); 80bl(Jaqui Hurst); 86tl(Ron Sutherland), r(Linda Burgess); 87tr(Linda Burgess), m(Vaughan Fleming); 92tr(Steven Wooster), bl(J. S. Sira); **Holt Studios Int.**: 30bl; 37br(Willem Harinck); 42tr(MichaelMayer); 60tr(Alan & Linda Detrick); 62bl(Primrose Peacock); 63tl(Bob Gibbons). **Houses and Interiors**: 88tr(Roger Brooks), bl(Roger Brooks); 89tr(Roger Brooks);**Hutchinson Library**: 8br(Robert Francis); 10tr(Merilyn Thorold); 13tr(Melanie Friend); 26bl(T. Moser), br(Lesley Nelson); 27tl(F. Horner); 28t(Edward Parker), bl (Sarah Errington), r(John G Egan); 29bl(Tony Souter); 38br(Hatt); 46bl(Tony souter); **Images Colour Library**: 11b; 12b; 13bl, bl; 14tr; 15no. 2, no. 5; 25br; 29tr; 36bl; 38t; 45,; 46r; 47bl; **The Interior Archive**: 8tl(Schulenburg); 9tr(Schulenburg); **Peter McHoy**: 61tl; 68tr; 76bl; 77tl; 82tl; 87tl. **The Stock Market**: 14br; 15no. 1(K. Biggs); 45; 46tr; 47t; Superstock: 22tr, m; 23br. View: 9m(Phillip Bier); 15no. 1(Dennis Gilbert); 45.

AUTHOR'S ACKNOWLEDGEMENTS

I should like to thank the staff at Anness Publishing Ltd: Helen Sudell for commissioning the book and Joanne Rippin for managing the project with courage and fortitude, despite the author, and Isobel for keeping her sane.

My family, as ever, deserve praise for their support and tolerance and the anonymous arm with the coffee mug at the end of it deserves a particular mention. Thanks to Tony Holdsworth and Jan Cisek for advice, and to all my friends for keeping off the telephone. A big thank you to Arto for being there and maintaining incredible patience – for a Fire Ox.

BIBLIOGRAPHY

Feng Shui (general)

Lau, Theodora, *The Handbook of Chinese Horoscopes* (HarperCollins, London, 1979)

Man-Ho Kwok, Palmer, Martin & Ramsay, Jay, *The Tao Te Ching* (Element, London, 1997)

Ni, Hua-Ching, *The Book of Changes and the Unchanging Truth* (Seven Star Communications, Santa Monica, 1983)

Palmer, Martin, *The Elements of Taoism* (Element, Shaftesbury, 1991)

Palmer, Martin, *Yin and Yang* (Piatkus, London, 1997)

Walters, Derek, *Chinese Astrology* (Aquarian Press, London, 1992)

Walters, Derek, *The Feng Shui Handbook* (Aquarian Press, London, 1991)

Wong, Eva, *Feng Shui* (Shambhala, Boston, 1996)

Understanding Feng Shui

Franz, Marie-Louise von, *Time* (Thames and Hudson, London, 1978)

Jung, Carl, *Man and his Symbols* (Arkana, London, 1990)

Lawlor, Anthony, *The Temple in the House* (G.P. Putnam's Sons, New York, 1994)

Lawlor, Robert, *Sacred Geometry: Philosophy and Practice* (Thames and Hudson, London, 1982)

Lindqvist, Cecilia, *China: Empire of Living Symbols* (Massachusetts, Reading, 1991)

Mann, A.T., *Sacred Architecture* (Element, Shaftesbury, 1993)

Pennick, Nigel, *Earth Harmony: Places of Power, Holiness and Healing* (Capall Bann, Chieveley, 1997)

Poynder, Michael, *Pi in the Sky* (The Collins Press, Cork, 1997)

Modern Feng Shui

Cowan, David & Girdlestone, Rodney, *Safe as houses? Ill Health and Electro-Stress in the Home* (Gateway Books, Bath, 1996)

Myers, Norman (ed), *The Gaia Atlas of Planetary Management* (Gaia Book Ltd., London, 1994)

Pearson, David, *The New Natural House Book* (Conran Octopus, London, 1989)

Thurnell-Read, Jane, *Geopathic Stress* (Element, Shaftesbury, 1995)

Gardens and Plants

Flowerdew, Bob, *Complete Book of Companion Planting* (Kyle Cathie Ltd., London, 1993)

Hale, Gill, *The Feng Shui Garden* (Aurum Press, London, 1997)

Harper, Peter, *The Natural Garden Book* (Gaia Books, London, 1994)

Hu Dongchu, *The Way of the Virtuous, the Influence of Art and Philosophy on Chinese Garden Design* (New World Press, Beijing, 1991)

Huntington, Lucy, *Creating a Low Allergen Garden* (Mitchell Beazley, London, 1998)

Liu Dun-zhen, *Chinese Classical Gardens of Suzhou* (McGraw Hill, Inc., New York, 1993)

Riotte, Louise, *Astrological Gardening* (Storey Communications Inc., Pownal, 1994)

Wolverton, B.C., *Eco-Friendly House Plants* (Weidenfeld & Nicolson, London, 1996)

Zhu Junzhen, *Chinese Landscape Gardening* (Foreign Languages Press, Beijing, 1992)

Ki Astrology

Sandifer, Jon, *Feng Shui Astrology* (Piatkus, London, 1997)

Yoshikawa, *Takashi The Ki* (Rider, London, 1998)

Space Clearing

Kingston, Karen, *Creating Sacred Space with Feng Shui* (Piatkus, London, 1996)

Linn, Denise, *Sacred Space* (Rider, London, 1995)

Treacy, Declan, *Clear your Desk* (Century Business, 1992)

INDEX